SPICE

First published in Great Britain in 2014
by Weidenfeld & Nicolson, an imprint of
Orion Publishing Group Ltd
Orion House, 5 Upper St Martin's Lane, London WC2H 9EA
An Hachette UK company

10 9 8 7 6 5 4 3 2 1

Text copyright © Dhruv Baker 2014
Design and layout © Weidenfeld & Nicolson 2014

A CIP catalogue record for this book is available from the
British Library.

ISBN: 978 0 297 87015 9

Photography by Kate Whitaker
Author photo, back cover by Simon Derviller
Design by Two Associates
Food styling by Lizzie Kamenetzky
Prop styling by Polly Webb-Wilson
Copy-edit by Clare Sayer
Proofread by Jennifer Wheatley
Index by Hilary Bird

Printed and bound in China

The Orion Publishing Group's policy is to use papers that
are natural, renewable and recyclable products and made
from wood grown in sustainable forests. The logging and
manufacturing processes are expected to conform to the
environmental regulations of the country of origin.

www.orionbooks.co.uk

Notes

All oven temperatures given are for conventional ovens. For
fan-assisted ovens reduce the temperature by 10°C or refer
to your oven manufacturer's manual.

All eggs are medium, unless specified. Use free-range eggs
where possible.

SPICE

LAYERS OF FLAVOUR

DHRUV BAKER

WEIDENFELD & NICOLSON

CONTENTS

INTRODUCTION

Spices are the foundation of and inspiration for much of my cooking and have been for years. I rely on them to add layers of flavour to my food, though this hasn't always been the case. There was a time when I was bewildered by the sheer number and complexity of spices. When you think of spice what comes to mind? Hot food? Curry? Confusion? All too often 'spice' or 'spicy' is used as a generic term, usually describing a dish which is particularly hot or that contains chillies. In fact, spices are wondrous, almost magical ingredients that, when used properly and balanced carefully, can help you to create a whole spectrum of extraordinary dishes, from the simple and delicate to the tantalisingly complex.

For centuries spices were one of the primary causes of war, exploration and empire building. They were hunted all over the globe and sent thousands of miles to royal courts as exotic bounties from far-flung, mysterious lands. We now have these exciting ingredients on our doorsteps – many of us have kitchen cupboards full of spices – and yet we tend to view them with a degree of confusion, if not suspicion. All over the country spices are bought, used once or twice and then consigned to the back of the cupboard for years. When they are finally used, they are merely faintly scented dust with little to offer – their magical properties having long since departed.

My spice cupboard is my haven, my treasure trove of flavour. I am inspired by the stunning aromas and flavours of spices, their amazing versatility and the opportunities they provide to add complexity to the food we cook. I want to share this love of spices with you and hopefully change the way you think about and use them.

Writing this now I can hear torrential rain on the windows and the grey street outside. But if I just imagine the smell of certain spices I am instantly transported to somewhere more exotic. The spring shower becomes the monsoon – warm, tropical and exciting instead of dreary and cold. This is the power of spice: harness that power and discover how they can lift your cooking to new heights.

MY KIND OF COOKING

My dad is English and my mum is Indian. I was born in Mexico, and when I was four years old we moved to India, where I spent the majority of my formative years. As a result it is the source of a large proportion of my culinary influences and treasured food memories. But I was also lucky enough to live in some other amazing places: Mexico, Spain, Tanzania and, of course, the UK. My recollections of my different homes are dominated by smells and flavours, each unique to wherever I was living at the time. It is the evocative nature of food that I find particularly fascinating. Whether it's tortillas cooking, the rich, heady scents of a bustling spice market, a huge paella over a wood fire or fish grilling at the local market, a single smell can unlock very specific memories for me instantly transporting me back to a particular time and place many years ago and many miles away. The food that I cook is the culmination of the experiences I've had, the places I've lived and the people I've met. As a family we used to take holidays and trips all over India, each of which contributed in some way to my love of and approach to food: eating lobster on the beach in Goa, steamed dumplings in the Kullu Manali Valley, crab *kalia* in Orissa or fish curries in Kerala. The smell of a barbecue being lit still conjures up visions of venison, wild boar, quail and pigeon cooked on a *sigri*, or brazier; pre-dinner nibbles being passed around as the kids drink mango juice and the adults enjoy far stronger stuff. Every time I cook my Mussalam lamb chops (see page 81), I'm suddenly back in my uncle's palace in Limbdi, Gujarat. I am constantly trying to recreate these food memories, often using them as starting points for new dishes.

I learned to love food at a very early age. My mum is the best cook I've ever known, even though she didn't cook at all when she was younger. Her family belongs to one of the former princely states of India. At the time of independence in 1947 her paternal grandfather was the last ruler of Kathiwada, a small state in Madhya Pradesh. Among his favourite pastimes was cooking, and his recipes are very much a part of our family's inheritance. My mother's maternal grandfather had two daughters. The elder, Princess Chandra Kumari, was my mother's mother. The younger, Princess Suraj Kumari, was married to Digvijay Singh, the Maharaja of Sailana (his book, *Cooking Delights of The Maharajas*, is still in print today). Throughout my mother's childhood all food was prepared in the palace kitchens, and as a result she never learned to cook. After she married my father, however, she started teaching herself. Now, 30 years later, she is responsible for some of the most stunning dishes I have ever eaten.

Food has always been very important to my family – both immediate and extended. My father's eldest sister, Yvonne, is an amazing cook and I remember clearly the vast spreads she would have waiting when we came over to the UK for the summer or weekend visits from school. This was my introduction to fantastic British home baking and cooking, food quite unlike that of my childhood. I can now appreciate that my style of cooking was beginning to take shape long before I was aware of it, and it is this foundation that I try to build on daily, influenced by new ingredients, techniques and recipes.

The dishes in this book are all linked by one common thread: spice. Because of this, it's very hard to label my style of cooking – I have always struggled with the concept of defining food strictly in geographical terms because a nation's food is a reflection of its past and history. The Spanish food that we enjoy today would have been very different if it had not been for the Moorish invasion, while Indian food before the arrival of the Portuguese would have lacked chillies, something almost inconceivable when we consider how prevalent they are to the cuisine now. For centuries the world over, cooking styles have evolved, developed, influenced and been influenced by other cultures and I like to think of my way of cooking in the same terms: the various influences coming together to create a constantly evolving way of looking at and cooking food. Similarly the traditional idea of dishes being either a starter, a main course or a side dish does not always apply and many of my recipes can be served in a number of ways: as one of several 'small plates', as a pre-dinner snack, a light lunch or as part of a celebration meal.

We have access to a limitless spectrum of ingredients and cuisines so why not take the elements we like most from each and see if we can't come up with something greater than the sum of the parts? This is how I love to cook and eat, which is reflected in the recipes in this book.

MY SPICE PHILOSOPHY

The best advice I can give anyone interested in cooking with spices is to understand the characteristics of individual spices. This will take time but trust me, it is time well spent. Read the section 'Unlocking the Spice Cupboard' on page 210, which explores the individual characteristics of the spices used in this book. Start by using one spice on its own (add cumin seeds to roast potatoes for example, or a cinnamon stick to a pork casserole or stew) and continue to experiment until you start to get a good idea of what kind of flavours and aromas different spices can bring to dishes. Once you are fairly confident using individual spices, you can start combining them.

Because spices can be so intense in flavour they possess the capability to ruin a dish if used in the wrong way, or to bring a dish to life if used in the right way. The recipes in this book will show you that each dish can have its own unique identity created by the subtle layering of flavours. See page 219 for different methods of cooking with spices, from dry roasting to infusing and making flavoured butters.

MY FLAVOUR MAP

When I taste a dish I immediately picture the flavours – almost like a visual map of what it is that I am eating. The more complex and flavoured a dish is, the more of the map is shaded in, the main flavour groups (sweet, sour, salty, savoury and bitter) taking up large areas, with the more subtle elements filling in the gaps.

The easiest way to explain this is to think of something really basic like chips and in your mind remove the salt. When you eat an unsalted chip it just feels incomplete and lacking in flavour. For me, my 'flavour map' is an extension of this, looking at all the ingredients in a dish and what they bring to it. Another way of trying to explain it is using the analogy of an orchestra. A piece of music can be performed using a single instrument – the piano. Then you bring in strings, percussion, woodwind, brass and before you know it you have something completely different. It's still the same piece of music but now it has staggering depth and richness. This is how I feel about spices – they are the additional sections of the orchestra, enhancing and enriching the original piece of music to make it more complex.

I adore food that changes slightly with each mouthful; the flavours evolving and developing, the subtleties coming and going like distant sounds shifting with the wind. This is where I believe spices come into their own. Taste is personal: a dish that is perfectly salty, sweet or structured for one person may not be so for another. For this reason, once you have tasted some of the recipes in this book you might want to add a bit more or less of one spice, or add or take away ingredients. You may find that some do not need altering at all, but however you use them, I hope that you will make them your own.

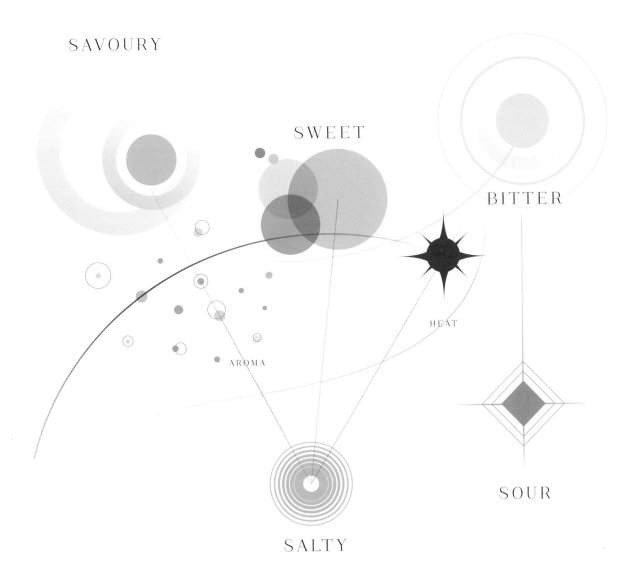

SAVOURY

SWEET

BITTER

HEAT

AROMA

SOUR

SALTY

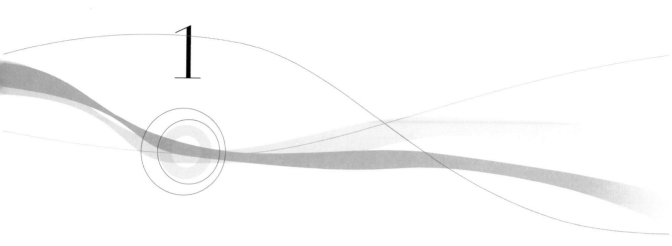

1

SMALL PLATES

SPICED PICKLED BEETROOT WITH GOAT'S CHEESE & HAZELNUTS

This recipe was inspired by a dish created by Atul Kochhar, a chef whom I admire enormously – he was the first Indian chef to win a coveted Michelin star. I love the big, bold flavours here: the earthy beetroot, sharp goat's cheese and the spices running throughout are held together by the sweetness from the sticky glaze.

Serves 4

For the pickling liquor
500ml ruby port
500ml malt vinegar
350ml water
350g caster sugar
5 star anise
1 vanilla pod
2 bay leaves
2 sprigs fresh thyme
2 tsp black peppercorns
2 tsp white peppercorns
1 blade mace
8 cloves

For the goat's cheese
200g mild rindless goat's
   cheese
1 tbsp vegetable oil
½ tsp brown mustard seeds
2 sprigs fresh curry leaves
1 tsp ground turmeric
50g plain flour
2 eggs, beaten
100g panko breadcrumbs,
   for coating
Oil, for deep-frying
Salt and freshly ground
   black pepper
4 medium raw beetroot,
   peeled and cut into
   wedges
50g toasted hazelnuts,
   roughly chopped
1 Granny Smith apple,
   cored and thinly sliced

Place all the ingredients for the pickling liquor into a large pan and bring to the boil. Turn down the heat and simmer until reduced by half, about 20–30 minutes, then add the beetroot and allow to simmer for 10 minutes until starting to soften. Take off the heat, cover and allow to cool completely.

Remove the beetroot and place in a container or dish. Strain the cooking liquor, discarding the spices, and pour half over the beetroot to stop it drying out. Return the other half to the pan and simmer for about 30 minutes until reduced by three-quarters. You should end up with a thick glossy syrup that coats the back of a spoon. Remember, this will thicken up when it cools.

Meanwhile, crumble the goat's cheese into a large bowl and set aside. Heat the vegetable oil in a frying pan and, when hot, add the mustard seeds and curry leaves. As soon as the mustard seeds start popping, pour the hot oil over the cheese. Add the turmeric and mix well with a spatula; season to taste. Place in the fridge to cool for at least 2–3 hours, ideally overnight.

Remove the cheese mixture from the fridge and roll into 12 equal-sized balls. Rub your hands with vegetable oil first – this will prevent the turmeric from staining and help you to create smoother spheres. Roll each one in the flour, then dip into the beaten egg and finally roll in the breadcrumbs until they are all coated. Return to the fridge until you are ready to deep-fry.

Pour the oil for deep-frying into a large, heavy-bottomed pan and heat to 190°C/375°F – a cube of bread dropped into the oil should sizzle and turn golden brown in about 20 seconds. Deep-fry the cheese balls, in batches if necessary, and set aside on kitchen paper to drain.

To serve, arrange the beetroot slices on a plate and scatter with the hazelnuts. Add the slices of apple and fried goat's cheese balls. Finally, drizzle over the reduced pickling liquor.

BUTTERNUT SQUASH WITH RED ONION, FETA & CORIANDER

The combination of sweet, roasted butternut squash, red onion and the tang of feta, offset by fresh coriander is one of my favourite flavour combinations. This warm vegetarian salad also works well as a light mid-week lunch or supper.

Serves 6 as a starter or
  4 for lunch

1 tsp coriander seeds
1 butternut squash, peeled,
  seeded and cut into
  4cm cubes
3 tbsp vegetable oil
2 sprigs fresh thyme
3 cloves garlic, unpeeled
1 red onion, finely sliced
150g feta, cubed
Juice of 1 lemon
50ml olive oil
Small bunch fresh
  coriander, roughly
  chopped
Salt and freshly ground
  black pepper

Preheat the oven to 180°C/350°F/Gas mark 4.

In a small pan, dry roast the coriander seeds, over a low heat, until they release their aromas. Allow to cool and then grind to a powder using a pestle and mortar or spice grinder.

Put the cubed butternut squash in a roasting tray with the vegetable oil and salt and pepper and toss to coat. Add the thyme sprigs and garlic cloves and cook in the oven for 20–25 minutes. After 10 minutes stir through the ground coriander seeds – I don't add them right at the start as they can burn and become bitter. Remove from the oven and allow to cool slightly. Remove and discard the thyme sprigs and set half the garlic aside.

Mix together the red onion and cooked butternut squash, then carefully stir in the feta cubes, taking care not to break up the cheese too much.

To make the dressing, squeeze half of the now softened garlic from the skins into a bowl and add the lemon juice and olive oil; whisk together. Pour the dressing over the butternut squash and scatter with the chopped coriander.

SPRING ONIONS WITH ROMESCO SAUCE

This dish takes its inspiration from Cataluña where calçots (Catalan spring onions) are a regional speciality. Traditionally, they are wrapped in newspaper, grilled over charcoal, the blackened outer layers discarded and the soft flesh dipped into romesco sauce. Spring onions are a good alternative. Any leftover sauce goes beautifully with grilled fish, chicken, lamb or asparagus.

Serves 4

For the romesco sauce
100g unskinned hazelnuts
6–8 cloves garlic, unpeeled
⅓ thin baguette, torn into
  chunks
2 tbsp vegetable oil
100g blanched almonds
150g fresh tomatoes
½ large red chilli, seeded
200g jarred roasted red
  peppers
Large pinch ground
  white pepper
50ml sherry vinegar
100ml olive oil
Juice of ½ lemon
Salt

16 spring onions or
  8 green onions
1 tsp olive oil
Pinch sea salt flakes

Preheat the oven to 200°C/400°F/Gas mark 6.

Put the hazelnuts in a frying pan and dry roast for 10 minutes. When cool enough to handle, rub them to remove the skins. You can, of course, buy skinned hazelnuts but I prefer to toast them as it gives a lovely smoky flavour to the sauce.

Place the garlic cloves and bread chunks in a bowl and drizzle with the vegetable oil, then place the garlic in a small roasting tin. Cook for 15 minutes before adding the bread chunks; cook for another 10 minutes until the bread is golden brown and the garlic softened. Set aside and when cool enough to handle, slip the soft garlic cloves out of their skins.

Whizz the hazelnuts and almonds in a food processor until finely ground. Add the bread chunks, garlic, tomatoes, chilli, red peppers and ground white pepper. It will be a thick paste now so add the sherry vinegar and keep the motor running as you drizzle in the olive oil. You'll end up with a glorious, thick, delicious sauce. If it's too thick, add a little water to thin down. Season to taste with salt and lemon juice.

Brush the onions with olive oil and sprinkle with sea salt flakes. Cook for couple of minutes on each side, either on a barbecue or in a smoking hot griddle pan. Arrange the onions on a platter and pour over the sauce.

AUBERGINE CRISPS WITH TRUFFLE HONEY

These pre-dinner nibbles featured on the bar menu during my chef's season at Benares (one of London's top Indian restaurants, headed by Atul Kochhar) proved very popular. Add a few spices to the breadcrumbs for extra flavour and then work out which version you like best – below are a few suggestions to get you going.

Serves 4

2 large aubergines, cut into
  thin slices, about 2–3mm
750ml whole milk
150g fine dried
  breadcrumbs
Coriander seeds, ajwain
  seeds or fennel seeds,
  coarsely ground
  (optional)
Oil, for deep-frying
50ml truffle honey or
  good-quality clear honey
Small bunch flat-leaf
  parsley, finely chopped
1 lemon, quartered
Salt and freshly ground
  black pepper

Put the aubergine slices in a bowl and cover with the milk – they should be submerged. Leave to soak for 1 hour.

Strain off the milk and discard and then use kitchen paper to pat off any excess moisture from the aubergines. Season the slices with salt and pepper.

Put the breadcrumbs in a shallow dish and stir in the coriander, ajwain or fennel seeds, if using. Coat each aubergine slice in breadcrumbs and set aside.

Heat the oil in a large, heavy-bottomed pan to about 180°C/350°F (the aubergine should sizzle as soon as it hits the oil). Deep-fry the aubergine slices in batches and drain on kitchen paper.

Serve the aubergine crisps drizzled with honey and scattered with chopped parsley. Finish with a squeeze of lemon juice.

FRIED BOCCONCINI

I'm a sucker for anything deep-fried. These balls of oozing, melting cheese served with a sharp and sweet relish really make my mouth water. Mozzarella is the perfect vehicle for the spices as it clings to all the wonderful flavours in the batter. If you can't get bocconcini, use regular buffalo mozzarella and cut into bite-sized cubes.

Serves 4

12 balls bocconcini or
  20 mozzarella pearls
25g rice flour
Vegetable oil, for
  deep-frying
1 lime, quartered
Tomato Relish (see page
  209), to serve

For the batter
125g rice flour
75g gram (chickpea) flour
2 tsp fennel seeds
½ tsp chilli powder
1 tsp ground turmeric
1 tsp ajwain seeds
¼ tsp garam masala
150–200ml cold water
Salt and freshly ground
  black pepper

Roll the bocconcini in the rice flour and leave in the fridge for a couple of hours or overnight.

Mix together all the ingredients for the batter in a large bowl, adding the water a little at a time until you have a thick, smooth batter.

Pour the oil for deep-frying into a large, heavy-bottomed pan and heat to 190°C/375°F – a cube of bread dropped into the oil should sizzle and turn golden brown in about 20 seconds.

Dip the flour-coated bocconcini into the batter then deep-fry, in batches, for 1–2 minutes. Remove and drain on kitchen paper.

Serve immediately with a squeeze of lime and some Tomato Relish.

CHEESE AND CUMIN CROQUETTES

One of my favourite Spanish tapas is 'croquetas' – cylinders of béchamel sauce, rolled in breadcrumbs and then deep-fried. Here I've added cumin seeds to give them a warming spice note. I often make these in large batches as they freeze really well – simply freeze the breadcrumbed croquettes on trays and transfer to freezer bags once they are solid. They will defrost in about 20 minutes so are perfect for serving with a glass of something cold the next time you have unexpected guests.

Serves 6–8 as a snack

750ml whole milk
2 bay leaves
1 onion, roughly chopped
1 tsp black peppercorns
6 cloves
100g unsalted butter
1 tsp cumin seeds
100g plain flour, plus extra
  for rolling
½ tsp ground cumin
200g grated Cheddar
  cheese
2–3 eggs, beaten
200g panko breadcrumbs
Oil, for deep-frying
Salt and freshly ground
  black pepper

Pour the milk into a pan and add the bay leaves, onion, peppercorns and cloves. Bring to a simmer then take off the heat and set aside to infuse for 5–10 minutes. Strain the milk into a jug and discard the spices and onion.

Melt the butter in a large pan and when foaming, add the cumin seeds. Stir-fry for a minute then add the flour and stir continuously over a medium heat for about 5 minutes, until golden. Gradually add the infused milk to the flour and butter, whisking to make sure you have a smooth mixture.

Stir in the ground cumin and cheese, season with salt and pepper and then pour into a bowl. Allow to cool, then cover with cling film and chill in the fridge for at least 3–4 hours. I often make this the day before and leave to chill overnight.

Use a tablespoon to scoop heaped portions of the chilled béchamel and then use your hands to roll into balls about the size of a walnut. A good tip is to rub your hands with a little oil to stop the mixture sticking to them. You should end up with 30–40 balls or croquettes.

Roll each ball in flour, then dip in beaten egg and finally roll in breadcrumbs. Heat the oil in a deep-fryer or large pan to 180°C/350°F, or until a cube of bread turns golden in 30 seconds. Deep-fry the croquettes in batches for 2–3 minutes until golden brown. Drain on kitchen paper and serve immediately with something to dip them into – try Saffron Aioli (see page 47) or some mayonnaise.

SMOKED SALMON, PINK GRAPEFRUIT & PICKLED CUCUMBER SALAD

Here the oily salmon and the fresh, sharp, bitter grapefruit seem worlds apart, but when bridged by the sweet and savoury miso and cucumber salad it all starts to make sense.

Serves 4

2 pink grapefruit

25ml olive oil

Juice of ½ lemon

Juice of ½ lime

½ large red chilli, seeded and finely chopped

1 large or 2 small fennel bulbs, tough outer layer removed

Small bunch fresh tarragon, leaves picked and finely chopped

200g smoked salmon, cut into strips

Small bunch fresh coriander, roughly chopped

Salt and freshly ground black pepper

For the miso-pickled cucumber

5 tbsp miso paste

100ml rice vinegar

3 spring onions, finely sliced

1cm piece fresh ginger, peeled and grated

150ml water

2 tsp sea salt

3 tbsp caster sugar

3 star anise

1 large cucumber, seeds removed and cut into very thin strips

Make the miso-pickled cucumber a few hours in advance, or even better a day or two earlier. Mix together all the ingredients except the cucumber in a large jar or airtight container and stir until well combined. Add the cucumber strips and set aside in the fridge for at least 3–4 hours so that they take on the flavours. This will keep in the fridge for up to a week.

Use a sharp knife to peel the grapefruit, including all the white pith. Holding the grapefruit over a bowl to collect any juice, cut the fruit into segments and place in a large bowl.

Mix the olive oil with 2 tablespoons of the collected grapefruit juice, lemon and lime juices, chilli and salt and pepper to make a dressing. Set aside.

Using a sharp knife or mandoline, slice the fennel as thinly as possible. Pour over half the dressing and sprinkle with the tarragon.

Arrange the fennel and the pickled cucumber on a plate and drape over the strips of smoked salmon. Scatter over the grapefruit segments and then pour over the rest of the dressing. Top with the chopped coriander and serve.

SALMON & SEA BREAM CEVICHE

There are few flavours more pronounced than within a ceviche – popular all over Central and South America. The acidity from the citrus not only cooks the fish but also cuts through the natural fattiness of salmon. Use the best and freshest fish you can find – you need sushi-grade fish for this dish.

Serves 6

250g skinless salmon fillet

250g skinless sea bream fillet

1 small red onion, finely sliced

Zest and juice of 1 lemon

Juice of 4–6 limes

Juice of ½ orange

1 tsp salt

½ tsp caster sugar

¼ tsp freshly ground black pepper

1 large red chilli, seeded and very finely chopped

1 ripe avocado, peeled and chopped into 1cm dice

Small bunch flat-leaf parsley

Small bunch fresh coriander

2 tbsp tequila (optional)

flour tortillas, quartered and shallow-fried or toasted sourdough, to serve

Place the fish fillets into the freezer an hour before you want to cut it – this will help keep them firm as you slice.

Plunge the sliced red onion into iced water and leave for about 10 minutes to lower the intensity of the flavour (if you do not do this the onion can overpower this dish). Drain and mix with all the remaining ingredients, except the fish. Set aside.

Remove the fish from the freezer and, using a very sharp knife, cut into 1–2cm slices, then cut the slices into 1–2cm strips and finally cut the strips into 1–2cm cubes. You can make the pieces smaller or larger if you would rather, but I love the texture you get this way.

Stir the fish cubes through the marinade and leave for between 30 minutes and 1½ hours. The lemon and lime juice will actually 'cook' the salmon but if you leave it too long the salmon can take on a chalky texture.

Serve the ceviche in small bowls with fried tortilla quarters or thinly sliced toasted sourdough.

SWEET CHILLI SQUID WITH SAMPHIRE

I will never forget the day I first tasted this dish. I was in Goa and had spent all morning with two chefs at the bustling and chaotic local markets, where I saw the most glorious fish. We bought everything we needed to cook a seafood extravaganza. After a few well-earned beers at the beach, we made a couple of starters to keep our appetites at bay while we prepared dinner, and this was one of them. Delightfully simple and cooked in seconds, it is utterly delicious. The samphire is not essential but it does add a lovely texture – if you can't get hold of it you could serve the squid with some wilted pak choi.

Serves 4–6

750g fresh squid (5–6 small
  squid is ideal)
75g cornflour
Oil, for deep-frying
100g samphire (optional)
15g unsalted butter
3 cloves garlic, finely
  chopped
1 tsp golden caster sugar
½ tsp chilli powder
1 lemon
Salt and freshly ground
  black pepper

Prepare the squid. First pull the tentacles away from the main body and then remove the beak from the centre of the tentacles. Carefully remove the quill (the almost plastic-like clear strip) from the body, then insert a thumb under the wings or fins and pull them away. Finally pull the membrane away from the body to leave a clean squid 'pouch'. Cut along one side of the pouch to create a flat piece of squid.

Using a very sharp knife, score diagonal lines across the squid at 5mm intervals to give a criss-cross pattern. Cut each squid piece into 3–4cm rectangles and slice the tentacles in half lengthways. Coat the squid pieces in the cornflour.

Heat the oil in a large, heavy-bottomed pan to 190°C/375°F (a cube of bread should sizzle and turn golden brown in about 20 seconds). Alternatively heat the oil in a deep-fryer. Deep-fry the squid in batches for about 2–3 minutes until crisp. Remove and drain on kitchen paper.

Cook the samphire, if using, in a large pan of boiling water or in a steamer for 1–2 minutes; drain.

Put a large frying pan over a medium heat and add the butter. When it starts to foam add the garlic and cook for 30 seconds before adding the sugar, chilli powder and salt and pepper. Add the drained samphire and squid pieces and toss in the butter.

Serve immediately with a squeeze of lemon.

CRAB CAKES

The combination of sweet crabmeat, spices and the zing of fresh herbs works together to give you these gorgeous nuggets of fried, crab deliciousness.

Serves 4

3 tbsp vegetable oil, plus
   extra for frying
1 cassia or cinnamon stick,
   split lengthways
5 cloves
5 green cardamom pods
1 star anise
2 tsp brown mustard seeds
1 banana shallot or 2 small
   shallots, finely chopped
2 tsp garlic and ginger
   paste (see page 215)
2 fresh green finger
   chillies, finely chopped
   (seeds are optional)
½ tsp ground turmeric
100g brown crabmeat
250g floury potatoes
   (Maris Piper or King
   Edward), peeled, boiled
   and mashed
150g white crabmeat
1½ tbsp finely chopped
   fresh coriander
1 tsp finely chopped
   fresh dill
1 lime
3 large eggs
3 tbsp plain flour
8 tbsp fresh white
   breadcrumbs
Salt and freshly ground
   black pepper
Tamarind Yoghurt (see
   page 207), to serve

Heat the oil in a frying pan, add the cassia or cinnamon, cloves, cardamom and star anise and fry over a medium heat for 4–5 minutes. Add the mustard seeds and when they start popping, add the shallots. Cook for a further 2 minutes. Stir in the garlic and ginger paste and cook for 1 minute.

Remove the cinnamon, cloves, cardamom and star anise and then stir in the chillies and turmeric. Reduce the heat to very low and add the brown crabmeat. Cook for a couple of minutes and then remove from the heat.

Transfer the mixture to a large bowl and add the mashed potato, the white crabmeat, coriander, dill and a squeeze of lime juice (save the other lime half for serving). Beat one of the eggs and add to the mixture; mix until well combined. Season to taste, then chill in the fridge for an hour or so, until firm enough to handle.

With wet hands, shape the mix into spheres – you should get 12 balls slightly smaller than a golf ball. Flatten them slightly and dust with flour. Refrigerate again for an hour to firm up (or make these up to a day in advance). Beat the remaining eggs. When ready to cook, dust the crab cakes in more flour, then the beaten egg and finally the breadcrumbs.

Pour the oil for frying into a large, heavy-bottomed pan to a depth of 5cm. Heat to 190°C/375°F, or until a cube of bread sizzles and turns golden in about 20 seconds. Deep-fry until golden and hot through, cooking in batches of three or four at a time. Drain on kitchen paper and serve with Tamarind Yoghurt and a squeeze of lime juice.

CHICKEN LOLLIPOPS

This recipe is dedicated to my uncle Lalji; he was the one who introduced me to chicken lollipops during a trip to Mumbai ten years ago. The tender chicken wings are marinated in an incredible mix of spices with a hefty kick of chilli. It may take a little time and practice to create the lollipop shape but I can't think of a better nibble to go with a cold beer.

Serves 6–8 as a snack

1kg chicken wings

Oil, for deep-frying

1 lime, cut into wedges

For the batter

100g plain flour

50g cornflour

4 tsp garlic and ginger
  paste (see page 215)

½ tsp red chilli powder

1 tsp paprika

2 green finger chillies,
  seeded and very finely
  chopped (for extra heat
  leave the seeds in one of
  the chillies)

½ tsp salt

½ tsp garam masala

Juice of 1–3 limes

1 tsp fennel seeds

½ tsp black pepper

First make your 'lollipops'. Use a sharp knife to separate the wings at the joint. You'll need only the biggest part of the wing so set the smaller two joints aside and use them to make chicken stock later. Take each large joint and, using a very sharp knife, scrape the meat towards the thick end of the joint so that you end up with meat at one end and a clean bone at the other end.

Mix together all the ingredients for the batter in a large bowl and beat until thick and smooth. Place the chicken lollipops in the batter and leave to marinate for 1–2 hours.

Put the oil in a large, heavy-bottomed pan and heat to 180°C/350°F – a cube of bread should sizzle and turn brown in about 20 seconds. Deep-fry the chicken, in batches, for about 5 minutes. Remove and drain on kitchen paper.

Serve immediately with lime wedges to squeeze over.

CHICKEN KOFTAS WITH CHILLI & CORIANDER DIPPING SAUCE

This recipe is a good example of my style of cooking. These chicken koftas are full of spice and the flavours are inspired by Indian, Thai and Mexican cuisine.

Serves 6 as a starter
(makes about 24)
500g minced chicken
2 tsp fennel seeds
4 tsp garlic and ginger
  paste (see page 215)
1 tsp ground turmeric
Juice and zest of ½ lemon
Juice and zest of ½ lime
1 red chilli, finely chopped
1 tbsp finely chopped fresh
  coriander
Vegetable oil, for frying
Salt and freshly ground
  black pepper

For the dipping sauce
100ml rice vinegar
1 tsp palm sugar
1 green finger chilli,
  seeded and finely sliced
1 tbsp finely chopped fresh
  coriander

Make up the dipping sauce, in advance if possible (a couple of hours is fine but the day before is even better). Mix all the ingredients together and leave in the fridge until you are ready to serve.

Put all the remaining ingredients, except the oil, in a bowl and mix until well combined. With slightly damp hands, roll the mixture into balls about the size of a golf ball. Mould them gently into oval shapes and then place in the fridge to chill for 1–2 hours.

Heat the oil in a frying pan and shallow-fry the koftas over a medium heat for 8–10 minutes, turning to brown on all sides. Drain on kitchen paper and serve hot with the dipping sauce.

CHINESE BARBECUE PORK PUFFS

Sweet, savoury, sticky and irresistibly moreish, the flavour of Chinese barbecued pork may well be one of the best out there. Encasing the pork in pastry makes the perfect canapé. This dish does require forward planning: you need to marinate the pork overnight, but you can make these in advance and freeze them – perfect if you are planning a party. Even better, they can be cooked from frozen; just add 5–7 minutes to the cooking time.

Makes 24

For the marinade
5 tbsp light soy sauce
5 tbsp dark soy sauce
5 tbsp clear honey
2 tbsp sugar
2 tsp Chinese five-spice
  powder
75ml rice wine or dry
  sherry
2 tbsp Hoisin sauce
2 tsp garlic and ginger
  paste (see page 215)

Whole pork belly, skin
  removed, about 500g
  (skinned weight)
2 x 500g all-butter puff
  pastry
2 eggs, beaten
1 tbsp sesame seeds
1 tbsp dark soy sauce
1 tbsp rice vinegar
1 green finger chilli, sliced
  (optional)

Put all the marinade ingredients into a small pan and heat gently until the sugar has dissolved.

Score the fat on the belly in a criss-cross pattern. Rub half the marinade all over the pork, making sure that the whole piece is well covered and that you have worked the marinade into the fat. Transfer to an airtight container and marinate in the fridge overnight.

Preheat the oven to 220°C/425°F/Gas mark 7. Put a rack inside a roasting tin that has a few centimetres of water in the bottom and place the pork on the rack. Cook in the oven for 15 minutes. Turn the meat over and rub over 1–2 tablespoons more of the marinade, reserving the rest for later. Reduce the oven temperature to 160°C/315°F/Gas mark 2½ and cook the pork for a further 2½ hours.

Remove the meat from the oven and allow to cool before cutting into 2.5cm thick slices, then chop each slice into small pieces. Stir the remainder of the marinade through the chopped pork and set aside.

Increase the oven temperature to 180°C/350°F/Gas mark 4.

Roll the pastry out to a thickness of a pound coin and then cut into 10cm squares. Place a heaped teaspoon of the filling into the centre of each square and then fold one corner of the square over to the opposite corner into a triangle. Brush the inside edges of the pastry with beaten egg and then seal all the way round with a fork.

When you have made all the puffs, brush the tops with beaten egg and sprinkle over a few sesame seeds. Bake in the oven for 20–25 minutes until golden.

Mix together the soy sauce, rice vinegar and chilli, if using, to make a dipping sauce for the puffs. Serve hot.

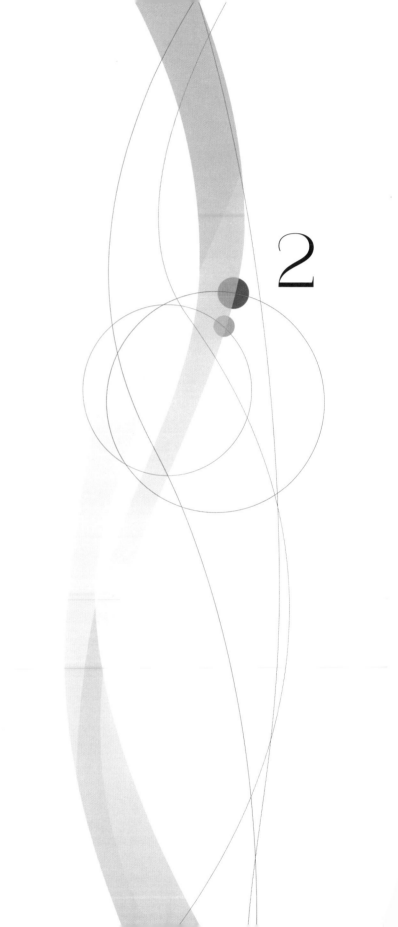

2

FISH

& SEAFOOD

TIGER PRAWNS WITH TOMATO & GARLIC

A few years ago in Portugal, I was served a dish that had piqued my interest long before it arrived at the table as I could smell it cooking in the kitchen! There were all sorts of familiar aromas – sweet, salty seafood, rich caramelised tomatoes, onions and garlic intertwined with a perfumed fragrance that I couldn't quite put my finger on. When the dish arrived, much to my surprise it was rosemary. Sweetness and acidity from the tomatoes and a wonderful kick from the garlic complemented the unmistakable flavour of this unexpected herb. It was divine. The next day I spent the morning trying to replicate the dish. Here is the recipe.

Serves 4

100ml olive oil

2 cloves garlic, finely sliced

1 ripe tomato, skinned, seeded and diced

½ tsp smoked paprika

2 sprigs fresh rosemary

300g raw tiger prawns, peeled but tails left on

1 lemon

Salt and freshly ground black pepper

Mix together the oil, garlic, tomato, paprika and rosemary sprigs in a bowl and add the prawns. Leave to marinate for 1 hour.

Put a frying or griddle pan over a high heat and, once hot, add the prawns, reserving the marinade. Cook for about 2 minutes each side or until cooked through.

Pour the reserved marinade into a small pan and bring to a simmer. Cook for 3–4 minutes until the garlic starts to change colour. This will cook the garlic but, more importantly, it's essential to do this as the oil previously had raw prawns in it.

Arrange the prawns on a large plate and pour over the flavoured oil. Season with salt and pepper and a squeeze of lemon juice.

GARLIC & CHILLI CLAMS

The beauty of this recipe is that you can serve it as it is with just a hunk of crusty bread or stir it through freshly cooked spaghetti to make a wonderful version of *spaghetti alle vongole*. Clams are delicious, inexpensive and quick to cook – this dish is ready in minutes!

Serves 4

1kg live clams

1 tbsp light olive oil

1 tbsp unsalted butter

1 banana shallot or
  2 shallots, finely diced

4 cloves garlic, finely sliced

1 large red chilli, seeded
  and finely chopped

50ml dry sherry (Palo
  Cortado adds a wonderful
  richness)

50ml white wine

Zest and juice of 1 lemon

Small bunch flat-leaf
  parsley, finely chopped

Salt and freshly ground
  black pepper

Rinse the clams well in cold water and scrub any that are particularly dirty. Discard any open ones and those which do not close when gently tapped against the worktop. I also tend to soak them in salted cold water for up to an hour as this helps purge any remaining sand; however if you are rushed for time don't worry about doing this.

Heat the olive oil and butter in a large pan and when it is foaming, add the shallots. Fry for 2–3 minutes then add the garlic and chilli and cook for another minute.

Add the clams and pour in the sherry and wine. Cover and cook for 3–4 minutes until the clams have all opened. Discard any that remain closed. Stir through the lemon zest and juice, parsley, season to taste with salt and pepper and serve.

MY FISH & CHIPS WITH MUSHY PEAS & BROWN SAUCE

I love a bit of humour in my cooking and this was my take on the nation's favourite, fish and chips, but with a kick of Indian flavour. The spices in this dish enhance rather than overpower the fish. You can use pretty much any firm white fish but my favourite has always been haddock.

Prepare the brown sauce. Put the tamarind pulp, water and sugar into a small pan and cook over a medium heat for about 15 minutes, stirring occasionally. Remove from the heat and then pass through a sieve to remove the seeds. Return to the pan and simmer until you have a thick, glossy sauce. Season with salt and pepper. You can make this 3–4 days in advance and store in an airtight container, in the fridge.

To make the mushy peas, put the split peas in a pan with the stock, onion, bay leaf and asafoetida. Bring to the boil, cover and simmer for 1 hour or until the peas have softened. Add the cooked frozen peas, coriander and mint, chilli and lime juice. This can be made a day or two in advance and simply reheated just before serving.

Mix together the garlic and ginger paste, salt, lime juice and chilli powder and rub the mixture all over the haddock fillets. Set aside in the fridge for 1 hour.

Put the fennel seeds, turmeric, ground coriander, ground cumin, mustard seeds, flour and baking powder in a bowl and mix well to combine. Add the cold water, a little at a time, and beat until you have a thick smooth batter.

Heat the oil in a deep-fryer to 150°C/300°F and fry the potato chips for 7–8 minutes. Set aside on kitchen paper.

Increase the temperature of the oil to 200°C/400°F. Coat each fish fillet in flour, dip into the batter mixture then carefully lower into the oil and deep-fry for 7–8 minutes, turning once or twice. Drain on kitchen paper and keep warm while you finish off the chips.

Return the chips to the deep fryer and fry for a further 5–6 minutes, until they are crisp and golden. Drain on kitchen paper and then toss in salt and the crumbled fenugreek leaves. Serve the fish and chips with the mushy peas and brown sauce.

Serves 4

2 tsp garlic and ginger paste (see page 215)
Pinch salt
Juice of ½ lime
½ tsp chilli powder
4 haddock fillets, about 750g in total
1 tsp fennel seeds
1 tsp ground turmeric
2 tsp ground coriander
½ tsp ground cumin
1 tsp brown mustard seeds
200g self-raising flour, plus extra for coating the fish
1 tsp baking powder
300ml ice-cold water
Oil, for deep-frying
4 large potatoes (Maris Piper or King Edward), peeled and cut into thick chips
1 tsp dried fenugreek leaves, crumbled
Salt and freshly ground black pepper

For the brown sauce
150g tamarind pulp
300ml water
3 tbsp caster sugar
Salt and freshly ground
   black pepper

For the mushy peas
100g dried split green peas
350ml vegetable or chicken
   stock
1 small red onion, finely
   chopped
1 bay leaf
Pinch asafoetida
100g frozen peas, cooked
2 tbsp finely chopped fresh
   coriander
1 tbsp finely chopped
   fresh mint
1 green finger chilli,
   seeded and finely
   chopped
Juice of 1 lime

MUSSELS IN GOA

One of my favourite places in the world is Goa. Beyond the moon parties and beach raves, the place offers such diversity of landscape, lifestyle and food. I spent many childhood holidays at local beach shacks, which were often nothing more than a roof on legs with plastic furniture to sit on and the sand to wiggle your toes in. But here you would always be guaranteed to eat the freshest seafood you'd ever find.

A few years ago, I went to Goa to explore the food culture and my starting point was Mapusa market. The main attraction was the fish stalls. Everywhere I looked there were fish of all shapes, sizes and varieties. It was here that I came across mussels being sold in a way I had never even imagined: rows of chattering old ladies in brightly coloured saris expertly removing the mussels from their shells at a phenomenal rate. They sold the mussels without their shells, in clear plastic bags. Once home, the cooking started. First off was a dish of mussels, which were marinated, coated in semolina and then deep-fried so that we had a snack to eat while cooking the rest of the meal – a civilised and sensible practice I heartily encourage.

DEEP-FRIED MUSSELS WITH SAFFRON AIOLI

Here, the mussels are steamed just enough to open the shells so you can remove the flesh easily before deep-frying. The textural contrast between the soft mussels and their crunchy exterior, with the heat from the chilli and the creaminess of the saffron mayonnaise make this a real standout dish. I have also used breadcrumbs instead of semolina for added crunch.

Serves 4

1kg live mussels

2 tbsp vegetable oil

1 shallot, finely chopped

50ml white wine

½ tsp fennel seeds

100g dried breadcrumbs

60g plain flour

2 eggs, beaten

Oil, for deep-frying

1 lemon

Salt and freshly ground
black pepper

For the saffron aioli

150ml good-quality
mayonnaise

Few strands saffron,
soaked in 2 tsp
warm water

1 clove garlic, crushed

1 tsp lemon juice

Pinch caster sugar

1 tsp finely chopped fresh
coriander

Rinse the mussels well in cold water and scrub any that are particularly dirty. Discard any open ones and those which do not close when gently tapped against the worktop. If any have rust-coloured fibres (beards) attached to them, pull these firmly away.

Heat the oil in a large pan, then add the chopped shallot and fry for a couple of minutes. Add the mussels and wine, stir thoroughly, cover and cook for 2 minutes or until the mussels open up.

Carefully remove the mussels from the shells, discarding any that remain closed.

Stir the fennel seeds into the breadcrumbs and season with salt and pepper. Toss the mussels in the flour, then dip in the beaten egg and finally in the seasoned breadcrumbs.

Heat the oil in a large, heavy-bottomed pan to 190°C/375°F, or until a cube of bread sizzles and turns golden in about 20 seconds. Alternatively use a deep-fryer. Deep-fry the mussels in batches for 1–2 minutes, then remove and drain on kitchen paper. Squeeze over some lemon juice.

Mix together the mayonnaise, saffron (with the soaking water), garlic, lemon juice, sugar and coriander and stir well to combine. Serve immediately along with the deep-fried mussels.

RAZOR CLAMS WITH SPICED CREAM

This is easily my most requested dish and I have never had anything but good reviews of it. It is inspired by Tom Kitchin, one of the most talented chefs I have ever had the good fortune to work with. While I was a stagiaire at his restaurant The Kitchin in Edinburgh, I learnt the proper way to prepare and cook razor clams, or 'spoots' as they are known in Scotland. These are the most wonderful example of seafood at its best. Sweet, beautifully textured and full of that wonderful salinity that quality seafood has – all complemented by the cream, turmeric, coriander and fennel in the sauce.

Serves 4

For the spice mix

½ tsp coriander seeds
½ tsp fennel seeds
½ tsp ground turmeric
¼ tsp garam masala
Pinch paprika
Pinch ground white pepper

2 tbsp olive oil
1 banana shallot or
  2 shallots, very
  finely chopped
2 cloves garlic, unpeeled
  but crushed with the flat
  blade of a knife
50g celeriac, peeled and
  very finely diced
50g carrots, peeled and
  very finely diced
12 large razor clams
  (rinsed well under cold
  running water)
100ml white wine
100ml double cream
Small bunch fresh
  coriander, roughly
  chopped
½ lemon

Make the spice mix. Using a spice grinder or a pestle and mortar, grind the coriander and fennel seeds. Mix in the ground turmeric, garam masala, paprika and white pepper, then set aside.

Heat the olive oil in a large, heavy-bottomed pan, and add the shallots, garlic, celeriac and carrots. Cook for a couple of minutes then add 2 teaspoons of the spice mix and fry for a minute. Add the razor clams, pour in the wine and stir for a few seconds. Cover and leave for about 1–2 minutes until the clams have all opened up.

Remove the clams from the pan using a pair of tongs, discarding any that have not opened. The clams should come away from the shells very easily but if not, use a teaspoon to tease them out. Using a sharp knife, cut off the solid white piece of muscle and discard the rest. Slice the clams and set aside. Place the shells in a pan of fresh water and boil for a couple of minutes to clean them. Set aside for serving.

Return the pan you cooked the clams in to the heat and bubble the liquid in the pan until it has reduced by a half to two-thirds – this should take about 10 minutes. Add the cream and cook for 5–7 minutes. Taste and adjust the seasoning, then add the chopped coriander and a squeeze of lemon juice. Stir through the sliced razor clams.

Arrange the cleaned and dried shells on four plates, allowing 2–3 shells per person. Serve the spiced clams in the shells.

HARISSA SARDINES

One of the most evocative smells has to be that of sardines cooking over a gentle wood fire. Fresh sardines – beautifully sweet with that gorgeous natural saltiness – are unbeatable. Harissa is a big, bold, potential bully of a flavour, but when used sparingly it is divine with fish. Cook the sardines on the barbecue or under a grill and serve with a wedge of fresh lemon and a sprinkling of chopped parsley.

Serves 6

12 fresh sardines, cleaned and gutted (ask your fishmonger)

2 tbsp harissa paste

4 tbsp olive oil, plus extra for serving

Small bunch flat-leaf parsley, roughly chopped

Juice of 2 lemons

Salt and freshly ground black pepper

Slash the sardines three or four times on both sides, season with salt and pepper and then rub thoroughly with the harissa paste. Drizzle with the olive oil and cook on a hot barbecue for 3–4 minutes each side or under the grill for the same amount of time (you may need a little less or longer depending on the size of the sardines).

Serve with the chopped parsley, a drizzle of olive oil and squeeze of lemon juice.

MALABAR PRAWN CURRY

This is one of those dishes that is as close to perfection as you can imagine. The balance of flavours is just right – coconut, mustard seed, curry leaves, ginger and tamarind – all working in harmony with the prawns. Just imagine eating this on a Goan beach with an ice-cold beer, wiggling your toes in the sand as you look out over the Arabian Sea. Heaven.

Serves 4

1 tsp tamarind pulp
2–3 sprigs fresh curry
  leaves, picked
1 tsp black mustard seeds
3 tbsp vegetable oil
½ tsp fenugreek seeds
2cm piece fresh ginger,
  peeled and grated
1 onion, finely chopped
¼ tsp chilli powder
1 tsp ground coriander
1 tsp ground turmeric
4–5 tomatoes, whizzed in
  a blender or ½ x 400g tin
  chopped tomatoes
100ml chicken or fish stock
600g raw prawns, peeled
400ml tin coconut milk
1 tbsp unsalted butter
Salt

Mix the tamarind pulp with a teaspoon of boiling water and pass through a sieve. Set aside.

Divide the curry leaves and mustard seeds equally between two separate bowls and set one of these aside for later.

Heat the oil in a pan and add one bowl of the curry leaves, the mustard seeds, fenugreek seeds and ginger and stir-fry for 30 seconds. Add the onion and cook, stirring regularly, for about 8–10 minutes, or until the onions start to turn a lovely golden colour.

Add the chilli powder, coriander and turmeric and stir-fry for another minute or two. Stir in the tomatoes and the tamarind paste and continue to cook for 10 minutes. Add the stock and simmer for about 20 minutes over a medium heat, until the liquid has reduced by half.

Add the prawns and cook for 5 minutes then reduce the heat to low. Add the coconut milk, cook for a further 2–3 minutes and then take off the heat.

Heat the butter in a small pan over a high heat. Once the butter is hot to the point of starting to smoke, add the remaining curry leaves and mustard seeds, which will instantly sizzle and pop. Tip the whole lot into the curry and stir through immediately – this is known as *tadka* or tempering, a widely used technique that adds flavour to finished dishes. Taste and adjust the seasoning and serve.

AJWAIN BATTERED POLLOCK

Ajwain, or carom, is a flavour I always associate with bhajis or bhajias, those crispy battered morsels you find on food stalls all over India. The options are endless – you can dip almost any vegetable into batter and deep-fry and you will not be disappointed. I've used fish but potato, cauliflower or onion would also work. The spiced and crisp batter goes perfectly with the creamy garlic aioli and the sharpness of the lemon to create a sublime harmony of flavours.

Serves 4–6

150g gram (chickpea) flour

50g self-raising flour

1 tsp salt

2 tsp ajwain seeds

1 tsp fennel seeds

½ tsp chilli powder

1 tsp ground turmeric

1 tsp ground coriander

2 tsp garlic and ginger
  paste (see page 215)

2 tbsp finely chopped fresh
  coriander

250ml cold water

Oil, for deep-frying

500g firm white fish fillets
  such as pollock or cod,
  cut into finger-sized
  strips

100g plain flour

1 lemon, quartered

Salt and freshly ground
  black pepper

For the garlic mayonnaise

150ml good-quality
  mayonnaise

1 clove garlic, finely
  crushed

1 tsp finely chopped fresh
  coriander

Mix together the gram flour, self-raising flour and salt in a large bowl, then stir in all the spices, the garlic and ginger paste and fresh coriander. Start adding the water, a little at a time, and whisk until you have a lovely, thick, smooth batter. Set aside.

Mix together the mayonnaise, garlic and coriander and set aside.

Heat the oil in a deep-fryer to 190°C/375°F; alternatively heat the oil in a heavy-bottomed pan until a cube of bread sizzles and turns golden. Season the fish strips then roll in the plain flour, dip in the batter and deep-fry in batches. Once cooked, drain on kitchen paper, squeeze over some lemon juice and serve immediately with the garlic mayonnaise.

MONKFISH WITH CHILLI & BLACK CARDAMOM

This dish is inspired by Hyderabadi cuisine, which is particularly close to my heart as I've always felt that Hyderabadi food is cooked with real gusto and love. This is a simplified version of a traditional fish dish; here I have used monkfish tail for its meaty texture and ability to carry spices. If you cannot find monkfish any firm white fish will also work. This is a perfect example of how cleverly balanced spices can deliver stunning flavours.

Serves 4

3 tbsp vegetable oil
6 cloves
3 black cardamom pods
2 large dried chillies,
  halved
1 onion, whizzed in a
  blender
2 tsp garlic and ginger
  paste (see page 215)
½ tsp chilli powder
1 tsp ground turmeric
150ml water
600g monkfish tail fillet,
  cut into 5cm chunks
1 lime, quartered
Salt and freshly ground
  black pepper

Heat the oil in a large frying pan over a medium heat and add the cloves, cardamom pods and dried chillies. Stir-fry for about 1 minute – don't allow the spices to burn otherwise your dish will end up tasting bitter.

Next add the onion and cook gently for about 10–12 minutes until very soft. The onions will deepen in colour as they start to caramelise.

Add the garlic and ginger paste, the chilli powder, turmeric and salt and pepper and cook, stirring, for another 2–3 minutes. Add the water and increase the heat. As soon as the liquid starts to bubble, add the monkfish pieces and turn a few times to coat in the spice mixture. Cover, reduce the heat to medium and cook for 8–10 minutes.

Use a slotted spoon to remove the cloves and the cardamom pods and discard. Serve the monkfish with the sauce spooned over the top and finish with a squeeze of lime.

PICNICS IN KATHIWADA

Kathiwada in Madhya Pradesh is a magical place that I visited many times as a child as it was the home of my grandfather. It was the picnics we enjoyed in Kathiwada that made this place so special to me. We drove for what seemed like an eternity and would eventually find ourselves in some beautiful, idyllic spot: by a stream under the mahogany trees, the floor decorated with the dappled light shining though the leaves as temporary kitchens were set up and bottles placed in the stream to chill. Or alongside a waterfall, the cool shade a wonderful respite from the long, hot, dusty drive. Here we would eat a wonderfully light and delicious red chicken curry; *pannias* – maize cakes cooked in a pit with hot coals and drizzled with clarified butter; *soolas* – venison or wild boar skewered and roasted on the braziers; and freshly caught river fish that were marinated and then cooked in a temporary tandoor oven, the smell of which I shall never forget. I have tried to recreate the flavour in the recipe that follows, which can be cooked in the comfort of your kitchen.

PAN-FRIED BREAM WITH FENNEL & TURMERIC BUTTER

Readily available, not too expensive and wonderfully delicate, bream is one of my favourite fish, though this spiced butter will work well with any white fish fillet. You can make the butter in advance as it will be happy in the fridge for a few days. Flavoured butters are a fantastic way to start introducing spices into your cooking as the butter helps to soften strong flavours which can otherwise overpower a dish. This is a great dish for a quick supper, served with a salad and some sautéed potatoes.

Serves 4

4 bream fillets, skin on
1 tbsp vegetable oil
Salt and freshly ground
  black pepper

For the flavoured butter
100g unsalted butter,
  softened
1 tsp fennel seeds
½ tsp ground turmeric
1 tsp garlic and ginger
  paste (see page 215)
¼ tsp garam masala
½ tsp ground coriander
½ green chilli, seeded and
  finely chopped
2 tbsp finely chopped fresh
  coriander
Zest and juice of ½ lime
Zest and juice of ½ lemon

Mix together all the ingredients for the flavoured butter except the lemon juice, making sure everything is thoroughly combined. Form into a sausage shape and wrap tightly in cling film. Chill in the fridge for at least 1 hour.

Check the fillets for any stray bones and remove any scales by scraping the skin with a sharp knife. Make three diagonal cuts in the skin of each fillet. Rub the skin side of the fillets with the vegetable oil and lightly sprinkle with salt.

Heat a non-stick frying pan over a low to medium heat. When hot, lay the fish fillets in the pan, skin-side down. Do not shake the pan, poke or prod the fillets or try to lift them for at least 7–8 minutes. You will know when it is time to turn the fish as there will be a golden halo around the edge of each fillet and the fish will have started to turn opaque almost all the way through.

While the fish is cooking, cut 3–4 slices of the flavoured butter, each about 2cm thick. It is far easier to cut through the cling film and remove this after you have cut the slices.

When it is time to turn the fish, increase the heat and carefully turn each fillet over to reveal the crisp, golden skin. Add the slices of butter, which will foam almost immediately. Carefully spoon the butter all over the fillets in the pan as you continue to cook for no more than 2 minutes.

Add the lemon juice, taste and adjust the seasoning and serve with the butter from the pan poured over the top of the fillets.

KEDGEREE

This is my take on that classic Anglo-Indian dish kedgeree. With just a couple of tweaks I have made this already fantastic dish even more special. It's incredibly easy and ideal for serving up to family or friends as a weekday supper. You can use regular hens' eggs in place of the quails' eggs if you can't find the latter.

Serves 4

1 litre chicken (or vegetable) stock
200ml whole milk
2 bay leaves
500g smoked haddock fillet
2 tbsp unsalted butter
1 large onion, finely chopped
2 cloves garlic, finely chopped
2 tsp mild curry powder
250g Arborio rice
8 quails' eggs or 4 hens' eggs
2 tbsp finely chopped chives
2 tbsp finely chopped flat-leaf parsley
Zest and juice of 1 lemon
Salt and freshly ground black pepper
Lemon wedges (optional), to serve

Put the stock, milk and bay leaves into a pan and bring to the boil, then immediately turn off the heat and slide in the haddock. Cover and allow to cook for 10–12 minutes. Remove from the pan and flake the haddock on to a plate, discarding the skin. Keep the warm milk to one side.

Meanwhile, melt the butter in a pan, add the onion and fry over a medium heat for about 10 minutes until soft but not coloured. Add the garlic and the curry powder, fry for another minute or two, then add the rice and stir to coat all the grains.

Start adding the stock and milk mixture in which you cooked the fish, adding a ladleful at a time and stirring until it is incorporated before adding the next ladleful.

Meanwhile, place the eggs in a pan of cold water and place over a high heat; as soon as the water boils, remove the pan from the heat. Leave the eggs to cook in the water – 7 minutes for hens' eggs and 2 minutes for quails' eggs. Plunge into iced water for 2–3 minutes, then peel.

When the rice is cooked, add the chives, parsley, flaked haddock, lemon zest and juice and salt and pepper. Stir through carefully so as not to break up the fish flakes too much.

Serve topped with the eggs cut into halves or quarters and a few lemon wedges.

LOBSTER POACHED IN FENNEL & SAFFRON BUTTER

This is the kind of dish that is perfect for a special occasion. The combination of garlic, ginger, fennel and saffron with the natural sweetness of lobster is hard to beat, but if you are feeling less extravagant, the lobster can easily be substituted for king prawns.

Serves 4

2 live lobsters weighing
   around 600–800g
100ml white wine
4 tsp fennel seeds
10 black peppercorns
250g unsalted butter
Few strands saffron
2 cloves garlic, thinly
   sliced
2 slices of fresh ginger,
   about the thickness of
   a pound coin
1 lemon, quartered
Crusty bread, to serve

Place the lobsters in the freezer for 20 minutes – this will make them docile and easier to cook.

Find your largest pan, fill with water and bring to the boil. Add the wine, 3 teaspoons of the fennel seeds and the peppercorns. Add the lobsters and boil for 10–12 minutes (you may need to cook them one after the other if you pan isn't big enough for both to fit comfortably).

Remove the lobsters from the pan and allow to cool slightly before twisting off the claws. Use a sharp knife to cut through the lobster tail and then remove the thin grey vein running along its length. Remove the meat from the tail and slice in half – you need to do this while it is still quite hot but not so hot that it is difficult to handle. Crack the claws using shellfish crackers or the back of a heavy knife and remove the meat in one piece.

Melt the butter in a pan and add the saffron, along with the remaining fennel seeds, garlic and ginger. Cook over a very low heat for 10 minutes; you want the butter to be gently bubbling as excessive heat will burn the spices, making the dish bitter.

Add the lobster meat to the butter and simmer gently for a couple of minutes.

Serve with crusty bread and a squeeze of lemon.

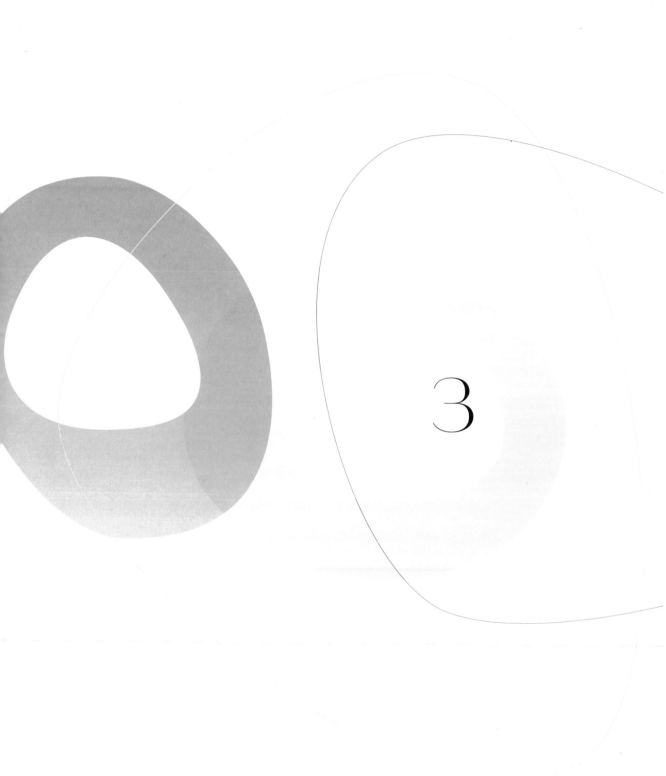

3

MEAT

PORK FRITTERS WITH ACHARI MAYONNAISE

In Hindi, *achari* means pickled – the spices used in this recipe are often found in Indian preserves. Here I've used a classic achari spice combination to make a delicious mayonnaise which goes perfectly with these spiced fritters.

Serves 4–6

175g panko breadcrumbs

1½ tsp fennel seeds

1½ tsp brown mustard
seeds

500g pork tenderloin,
cut into 2cm slices and
flattened with a knife

25g plain flour, seasoned

2 eggs, beaten

Oil, for deep-frying

Salt and freshly ground
black pepper

For the achari mayonnaise

2 tsp fennel seeds

½ tsp nigella seeds

½ tsp brown mustard seeds

½ tsp fenugreek seeds

3 tbsp vegetable oil

2 whole dried red chillies

3 cloves garlic, crushed

5cm piece fresh ginger,
peeled and grated

Pinch asafoetida

½ tsp chilli powder

1 tsp ground turmeric

½ tsp garam masala

Pinch salt

150ml good-quality
mayonnaise

First make the spice mix for the achari mayonnaise. Coarsely grind the fennel, nigella, mustard and fenugreek seeds in a pestle and mortar to make a spice mix. Heat the oil in a frying pan and add the dried red chillies, garlic and ginger. Stir-fry for 1 minute. Add the asafoetida along with the spice mix. Stir-fry for a further minute.

Add the chilli powder, turmeric, garam masala and salt and cook for 1 minute with a couple of tablespoons of water to prevent it sticking and burning. Remove from the heat and allow to cool. Take out the red chillies and then stir 1½ teaspoons of the spice mix through the mayonnaise. Set aside.

Mix together the breadcrumbs, fennel and mustard seeds and season with a pinch of salt and pepper. Dust the pork slices in the flour, dip in the beaten egg and then in the breadcrumbs.

Heat the oil in a deep-fryer or large, heavy-bottomed pan to 190°C/375°F – a cube of bread should sizzle and turn golden in 20 seconds. Deep-fry the pork fritters, in batches, for 2–3 minutes until they are crisp and golden. Remove and drain on kitchen paper. Serve immediately with the achari mayonnaise.

YELLOW PORK

My mum has cooked this for as long as I can remember and for me, it represents everything that good comfort food should be. It is incredibly easy to cook and you will be astounded at the end result – tender chunks of pork coated in a richly spiced yoghurt. Called yellow pork because of the turmeric, which gives it a lovely golden colour.

Serves 4

500g pork shoulder or leg,
  cut into 3–4cm cubes
500g Greek yoghurt
2 large onions, very finely
  sliced
4 tsp garlic and ginger
  paste (see page 215)
2 tsp ground coriander
1 tsp ground cumin
2 tsp ground turmeric
6 large dried red chillies,
  seeds removed
Salt and freshly ground
  black pepper

Mix all the ingredients except the dried chillies together in a large, lidded ovenproof dish. Place over a medium to high heat and bring to the boil, stirring occasionally. Once the whole lot is simmering away happily, pop the lid on, turn the heat right down and leave to cook for 30–40 minutes, stirring every 5–10 minutes. Add the dried chillies and cook for a further 30 minutes.

Remove the lid and cook for a further 30 minutes, stirring regularly until most of the liquid has evaporated. You should be left with a thick, creamy sauce coating the pork, which will be practically falling apart.

Serve with rice or hot-buttered naan breads. This is also delicious with a fresh, zingy Kachumber (see page 204).

THE BEST SPARE RIBS EVER

I have always been a sucker for spare ribs – they are devastatingly moreish! This recipe will show you how to achieve beautifully tender ribs, coated in the most gorgeous spice mix. If you have any leftovers, strip all the meat off the bones and use the following day as a filling for sandwiches.

Serves 4 as a main or
  8 as a starter

For the marinade

5 tsp fennel seeds

3 tsp black peppercorns

2 tsp coriander seeds

4 tbsp vegetable oil

1 large onion, whizzed
  in a blender

4 cloves garlic, crushed

3cm piece fresh ginger,
  peeled and grated

2 tsp smoked paprika

100ml cloudy apple juice

50ml maple syrup

1 tbsp English mustard

4 tbsp demerara sugar

100ml ketchup

20ml brown sauce

50g apricot jam

100ml water

Pinch salt

2kg pork belly ribs

2 tbsp caster sugar

3 tbsp malt vinegar

1 tsp Tabasco

Start by grinding the fennel seeds, black peppercorns and coriander seeds using a spice grinder or pestle and mortar until you have a fine powder.

Heat the oil in a large frying pan over a medium heat and add the blended onion along with the ground spices. Fry for 10–12 minutes, or until the onion starts to brown slightly. Add the garlic and ginger and cook for a further 5 minutes.

Add all the remaining marinade ingredients and cook, stirring every couple of minutes, for 15–20 minutes. You should end up with a gorgeously thick, glossy and fragrant sauce. Take off the heat and allow the sauce to cool then rub over the ribs and leave to marinate for as long as possible (overnight is ideal but an hour or two will do if you don't have the time).

Preheat the oven to 140°C/275°F/Gas mark 1.

Place the ribs in a deep roasting tin and cover tightly with foil. Cook in the oven for 3–4 hours until the meat is meltingly tender but still holding on to the bones.

Remove from the oven, and pour the juices from the roasting tin into a small pan. Bring to the boil and then whisk in the sugar, vinegar and Tabasco. Reduce the heat and simmer for 10 minutes, or until the sauce has reduced by about one-third.

If you want to finish the ribs on the barbecue, place them over the hot coals and cook for 5 minutes, turning once or twice and basting with the finished sauce. If finishing in the oven, preheat the oven to 220°C/425°F/Gas mark 7, smother the ribs in some of the sauce and cook for 10–12 minutes, until the sauce starts to caramelise.

Serve with the rest of the sauce to dip the ribs into.

PORK PIBIL

The taste of pork pibil instantly takes me back to being in the Yucatán, Mexico. I remember eating this for the first time in 1999 in Merida – one of my favourite cities on earth – during one of the many *ferias*, or local holidays. Pork laden with spices, topped with pickled red onions and wrapped in a tortilla – it was proper street food, the best way to experience the food of any city.

Serves 6

For the spice mix
3 tsp cumin seeds
4 tsp fennel seeds
1 tbsp black peppercorns
½ tsp cloves
1 tsp crushed dried red
  chillies
2 tsp hot-smoked paprika
1 tsp ground cinnamon
2 tsp ground allspice

For the pickled red onions
300ml white wine vinegar
130ml water
100g caster sugar
1 star anise
1 cinnamon stick
2 red onions, thinly sliced

For the marinade
1.25 kg pork shoulder,
  cut into 5–7cm cubes
50ml white wine vinegar
Juice of 2 oranges
Juice of 2 lemons
4 cloves garlic, crushed
25ml tequila
2 tsp salt

To serve
Corn or flour tortillas
1–2 ripe avocados, stoned
  and sliced
Bunch fresh coriander,
  torn
1–2 tomatoes, sliced

Grind all the whole spices for the spice mix to a fine powder using a pestle and mortar or spice grinder. Stir in the paprika, ground cinnamon and ground allspice.

Put the cubed pork shoulder in a large bowl and mix through half the spice blend (keeping the other half in an airtight container for another time), making sure all the pieces are covered. Stir in all the remaining marinade ingredients, cover with cling film and leave to marinate in the fridge for 2–3 hours, ideally overnight.

Pre-heat the oven to 160°C/315°/Gas mark 2½.

Put the pork along with the marinade into a deep roasting tin and cover tightly with foil. Transfer to the oven and cook for 3 hours until soft and tender.

To make the pickled red onions, add the vinegar, water, sugar, star anise and cinnamon to a pan and bring to the boil. When the liquid comes to the boil add the sliced red onions and immediately take off the heat. Allow to cool before serving. These can be kept in an airtight container in the fridge for a couple of weeks.

Remove the pork from the oven and shred the pieces using two forks. Serve wrapped in corn or flour tortillas with sliced avocado, fresh coriander, sliced tomatoes and the pickled red onions.

SLOW-ROASTED PORK BELLY WITH FENNEL & CORIANDER

This is my favourite Sunday lunch. There is nothing more satisfying than putting a whole pork belly in the oven to cook slowly for several hours while you go for a long walk somewhere. The trick is to cook the pork at a low temperature, giving the meat time to soften and the fat to render out, making perfect crunchy crackling. Fennel and pork are old friends but I have added coriander seeds as well, because the citrus note works beautifully with the fennel.

Serves 4–6

2 tsp fennel seeds
2 tsp coriander seeds
½ tsp black peppercorns
1.5kg whole pork belly,
  boned and trimmed
2 tbsp vegetable oil
1 tsp sea salt flakes
1 bunch fresh thyme
2 bay leaves
500ml water

Preheat the oven to 140°C/275°F/Gas mark 1.

Roughly crush the fennel seeds, coriander seeds and peppercorns using a pestle and mortar or spice grinder and set aside.

Using your sharpest knife (it may be worth investing in a craft knife for this), score the skin of the pork belly very finely all over, creating lines about 1cm apart. You might want to ask your butcher to do this for you.

Rub the skin with vegetable oil then sprinkle over the sea salt and ground spices. Use your hands to really work the salt and spices into top and bottom of the joint.

Put the thyme, bay leaves and water in a deep roasting tin and place a rack inside. Put the pork belly on the rack, making sure that there is a small gap between the water and the pork. Cook in the oven for 5–6 hours, topping up every now and then with water if necessary.

Remove from the oven and leave to rest for 20 minutes before carving. The meat should be very tender and the skin golden and crunchy.

PORK CHOPS WITH FENNEL, GARLIC, THYME & LEMON

This is one of my go-to barbecue dishes but these marinated chops can also be baked in the oven. However you cook it, the key is to use good-quality pork and to make sure you allow several hours (overnight is best) for it to wallow in that delicious marinade.

Serves 4

4 large pork chops
50ml light olive oil, plus
    extra for drizzling
3–4 sprigs fresh thyme
2 tsp fennel seeds
3–4 cloves unpeeled garlic,
    bashed with the flat of
    a knife
1 lemon, halved
Salt and freshly ground
    black pepper

Using a knife, make 3–4 small cuts in the fat of each chop – this will help the flavours permeate and allow the fat to cook out.

In a bowl, mix together the oil, thyme, fennel seeds, garlic, the juice of one lemon half and some black pepper. Add the pork chops, turn to coat in the marinade, cover and leave in the fridge for a few hours, preferably overnight.

Preheat the oven to 180°C/350°F/Gas mark 4.

If cooking in the oven, arrange the chops in a baking tray, pour over the marinade and cook in the oven for 30 minutes, or until cooked through and golden.

If cooking on the barbecue, cook as above but remove the chops from the oven after 15 minutes. Place on a hot barbecue and cook for 5–6 minutes, turning occasionally, until cooked through.

Season with salt and pepper, squeeze over the remaining lemon and serve with sautéed potatoes. My Caponata (see page 142) also makes a good accompaniment.

FISHING AND SHOOTING IN LIMBDI

If I think of some of the food I still love to eat now I can trace a fair deal back to Limbdi, where I spent many family holidays and made a real connection with meat and fish. I was taught how to fish and shoot, and how to gut and clean what we had caught. We would hunt for duck at sunrise and play in the back of an uncomfortable Willis Jeep for hours. Fishing expeditions meant long afternoon picnics by lakes and rivers, joking around and drinking hot tea. All that was caught or shot was always taken home and cooked, then eaten by the whole family around a huge table.

Limbdi was, and still is, somewhere very close to my heart. A beautiful palace with marble turrets and vast balconies with acres to roam and explore. My brother, cousins and I would wander the grounds for hours as if we were on an epic journey of discovery and then return to the house for a pre-dinner snack on the veranda. I looked forward to these meals of marinated meat and game cooked on the brazier and served with a squeeze of lime, including delicate lamb kebabs, the meat worked with a stone to give a beautifully smooth texture. Loving family, good friends, lots of laughter and wonderful food – the vital components to happiness, in my opinion.

Mohan, my aunt and uncle's long serving cook and his less than efficient side-kick, Versuba, tirelessly turned out meal after meal to this voracious crowd. To this day I can remember the flavour of his lamb chops, which I have experimented with time and time again.

MUSSALAM LAMB CHOPS

This is truly worth every second of the time it takes to prepare. I cooked this dish for the Maharajah of Jodhpur, a renowned gourmand, and was understandably nervous! You will be pleased to know that the Maharajah ordered more lamb, the highest compliment possible, so naturally I had to include the recipe in this book.

Serves 4

For the sauce

4 tbsp vegetable oil
1 onion, thinly sliced
10 tbsp Greek yoghurt
½ tsp chilli powder
4 tsp ground coriander
1 tsp garam masala
½ tsp coarsely ground
   black pepper
2 tbsp gram (chickpea)
   flour
1 tsp ground ginger
5 green cardamom pods,
   lightly crushed to extract
   the seeds
1 blade mace
½ tsp salt
Few strands saffron,
   soaked in 2 tbsp hot
   water
100ml water or lamb stock

2 trimmed lamb racks
1 tbsp unsalted butter
1 tbsp vegetable oil

Preheat the oven to 200°C/400°F/Gas mark 6.

For the sauce, heat the oil in a pan and fry the onion over a medium heat until golden, about 10–15 minutes. Remove from the pan, drain on kitchen paper and then transfer to a food processor along with the remaining sauce ingredients, except the water or stock, and whizz for a few seconds. Transfer to a pan and cook over a medium heat for 20 minutes, stirring every few minutes so that it doesn't stick or burn. Add the water or stock and stir through.

Score the fat on each rack with a sharp knife in a criss-cross pattern, making cuts about 1cm apart.

Place the racks fat side down into a dry frying pan over a low heat and leave for about 10 minutes until most of the fat has rendered out. Pour away the fat, turn up the heat and sear the meat all over (this will take 2–3 minutes).

Place the racks in a roasting tray and spoon over enough of the sauce to coat. Roast in the oven for 10–12 minutes. Remove the racks and slice into chops.

Melt the butter and tablespoon of oil in a frying pan and fry the chops for 1 minute on each side. Add the remaining sauce and heat through for a couple of minutes. Serve with Cumin and Chilli Potatoes (see page 145) and Kachumber (see page 204) along with some flat breads to mop up the juices.

LAMB AND LENTIL SHAMI KEBABS

This is a real standout dish – the hint of the chilli, warmth of the ground spices and spikes of freshness from the coriander and lime are all set against the smooth texture of these kebabs. My mother has made these for years – I ask her to cook them pretty much every time I go to hers for a meal. As the story goes, a chef created them for a toothless Nawab of Luknow who needed the kebabs to be so silky fine that they required no teeth to be eaten.

Serves 4–6

200g chana dal
2 tsp ginger paste (see page 215)
6 cloves garlic
2 green finger chillies, finely chopped (leave the seeds in for more of a kick)
1kg lean lamb mince
2 cinnamon sticks
3 black cardamom pods
1 bay leaf
½ onion, studded with 8 cloves
800ml cold water
2 eggs, beaten
1 tsp garam masala
Small bunch fresh coriander, roughly chopped
100ml vegetable oil
Lime wedges, to serve
Salt and freshly ground black pepper

Soak the chana dal overnight in plenty of cold water.

Put the ginger, garlic, chillies, lamb mince, drained chana dal, cinnamon sticks, cardamom pods, bay leaf and clove-studded onion into a large pan and pour over the cold water. Place over a medium to high heat and bring to the boil. Reduce the heat to a simmer and cook for about 45 minutes to 1 hour, or until all the water has evaporated.

Allow to cool slightly, remove the whole spices then whizz the mixture in a food processor until you have a chunky paste. Add the eggs, garam masala and coriander and stir well to combine. Taste and season with salt and pepper.

Wet your hands with a little water and roll the mixture into spheres about the size of a golf ball. Flatten them slightly to get smooth patties about 1–2cm thick. Place in the fridge to chill for at least 2 hours, or overnight if possible.

Heat the oil in a frying pan or wok over a medium heat. Fry the patties in batches for about 90 seconds on each side – be very careful when turning them as they are delicate and break easily. Drain on kitchen paper and serve immediately with lime wedges. This is even more special served with Mint and Coriander Yoghurt (see page 206).

BRAISED SHOULDER OF LAMB WITH RAS EL HANOUT

This meltingly tender lamb, infused with the wonderful aromas of Morocco and served with couscous and a drizzle of honey, is the perfect food for tucking into with family and friends.

Serves 6–8

2.5 kg shoulder of lamb,
  on the bone
2 tbsp ras el hanout
50ml light olive oil
2 large onions, roughly
  chopped
1 bunch fresh thyme sprigs
5–6 cloves garlic, unpeeled
3 tbsp clear honey
Salt and freshly ground
  black pepper

For the couscous
350g couscous
1 chicken stock cube
1 small red onion, finely
  chopped
10–12 cherry tomatoes,
  quartered
2 tbsp raisins
2 tbsp flaked almonds
2 tbsp freshly chopped
  flat-leaf parsley
2 tbsp freshly chopped
  coriander
Juice of ½ lemon
2 tbsp olive oil
Salt and freshly ground
  black pepper

Prick the lamb all over with a skewer or a sharp knife. Mix together the ras el hanout, olive oil and salt and pepper and rub all over the lamb shoulder (this is best done the day before to maximise the flavours but a couple of hours before will suffice).

Preheat the oven to 140°C/275°F/Gas mark 1.

Place the chopped onions, thyme sprigs and garlic cloves in a roasting tin or ovenproof dish and sit the lamb on top. Cover tightly with foil and put in the oven for 4–5 hours. Check every hour or so to make sure the onions and garlic are not burning (if they are then reduce the heat slightly). Drain off the fat in the roasting tin every couple of hours. Remove the foil and cook uncovered for the last 45 minutes.

Meanwhile, tip the couscous into a large bowl and crumble in the stock cube. Pour over 400ml boiling water, stir quickly and then cover tightly with cling film. Leave for 5 minutes and then use a fork to fluff up the grains. Stir through the remaining ingredients and then taste and adjust the seasoning.

Lift the lamb out on to a clean chopping board and use two forks to shred the meat off the bone. Pile the couscous into the centre of a large serving dish, arrange the shredded lamb on top and drizzle over the honey.

SPICED LAMB & CORIANDER WRAPS

Easy to put together and packed full of flavour, this is just the kind of dish I love to make for lunch. Based on a recipe from my childhood (given to me by my dear friend Jake), the lamb mixture was originally served in warm pitta, but I prefer it in large flour tortillas to catch all the bits of filling that seem to fall out of pitta breads.

Serves 4–6

3 tbsp vegetable oil
1 large onion, finely chopped
2 cloves garlic, chopped
1 tsp ground cumin
Pinch ground nutmeg
500g lamb mince
Large bunch fresh coriander, roughly chopped
3–4 bird's eye green chillies (depending on how much heat you like), finely chopped
2 limes
4–6 large flour tortillas
Salt and freshly ground black pepper

Heat the oil in a large frying pan over a medium heat. Add the onion, stirring to prevent it catching and burning. Cook until it turns pale gold in colour, about 7 minutes, then add the garlic and cook for a further 2 minutes before adding the cumin and nutmeg. Cook for a further minute.

Turn up the heat and add the mince, breaking up any large lumps with a wooden spoon. Cook for about 10 minutes until nicely browned and until any excess water has disappeared.

Add the coriander, chillies, salt and pepper and the juice of one lime and stir well to combine. Serve in the tortillas with extra lime juice squeezed over, if desired.

THAI VEAL SALAD

Thai salads, more often than not, are about creating a balance of chilli heat, sweetness, sourness, saltiness and texture. This is a dish to send your taste buds into overdrive with its brave, bold flavours. Veal works well as it is slightly sweeter and more delicate than beef.

Make the dressing a few hours in advance to let all the flavours develop. Mix together all the ingredients in a small jug or bowl and set aside. This will keep in the fridge in an airtight container for up to 1 week.

If you are using veal fillet, preheat the oven to 200°C/400°F/Gas mark 6. Rub the fillet all over with the vegetable oil and the salt, then sear on all sides in an extremely hot griddle pan – give each side a minute before turning. Transfer to a small roasting tin and cook in the oven for 10–12 minutes. Remove from the oven and allow to rest for at least 15 minutes before cutting into very thin slices.

If you are using escalopes, rub them with oil and salt and cook in a hot griddle pan for 1 minute on each side. Allow to rest for 5 minutes, then slice into 5cm strips.

To assemble, place the veal slices or strips in a large shallow bowl and coat with the dressing. Add all the remaining ingredients except the peanuts, coriander leaves and lime halves and mix well with your fingers. Just before serving, scatter over the peanuts and coriander leaves and squeeze over the lime juice.

Serves 4

500g veal fillet or 4 x 125g escalopes

1 tbsp vegetable oil

1 tsp sea salt

½ head white cabbage, very finely sliced

1 large carrot, grated or cut into long strips

1 red onion, very finely sliced

150g beansprouts

Small bunch fresh coriander, roughly chopped

1 tbsp roughly chopped fresh mint leaves

½ lemongrass stalk, outer layer removed and very finely chopped

25g dry-roasted peanuts, crushed

4 tbsp whole coriander leaves

1 lime, halved

For the dressing
Juice and zest of 1 lime
1 tbsp palm sugar
1 tbsp groundnut oil
1 tbsp fish sauce
1 tsp sesame oil
5cm piece fresh ginger,
    peeled and finely grated
1 tbsp kecap manis
    (alternatively use dark
    soy sauce with a pinch of
    sugar)
1 tbsp light soy sauce
1 clove garlic, crushed
1–2 red chillies, finely
    sliced
50ml water

WIENER SCHNITZEL WITH PAPRIKA & MUSTARD MAYONNAISE

We all have dishes that we fall back on when we need a little bit of a lift and this is one of mine – it's very easy to prepare and cooks in minutes. I absolutely adore veal and the mustard and paprika work well with the delicate flavour of the meat.

Serves 4

4 veal escalopes, about 100–150g each
50g plain flour
1 tsp paprika
100g white breadcrumbs
3 eggs
100ml vegetable oil
2 tsp hot German mustard (or use 50:50 French and English)
100ml good-quality mayonnaise
1 lemon, quartered
Salt and freshly ground black pepper

Lay the veal escalopes out on a clean chopping board and cover with a layer of cling film. Use a rolling pin and tap gently to flatten them out.

Season the flour with salt and pepper, stir in half the paprika and spread out on a baking tray. Tip the breadcrumbs into a second baking tray, add the remaining paprika and stir through. Break the eggs into a shallow bowl, big enough for the escalopes to fit into one at a time, and beat well.

Coat each veal escalope in the flour, then dip in the egg and coat thoroughly in the breadcrumbs.

Heat the oil in a large frying pan and while it is heating mix together the mustard and mayonnaise; set aside. Shallow-fry the escalopes two at a time – they should take no more than 2–3 minutes for each side. Drain on kitchen paper and keep warm while you cook the remaining escalopes.

Serve immediately with a squeeze of lemon, the mustard mayonnaise, some sautéed potatoes and a green salad.

HOMEMADE SALT BEEF

Making your own salt beef is one of the single most satisfying things you can do, akin to making your own sausages or baking your own sourdough, but happily it is much easier than either of those. Essentially this is a curing process so it will take a bit of time, however by taking on the flavours of aromatic spices a humble piece of brisket is transformed into a delicious, meltingly tender thing of beauty. Serve with Choucroute (see page 207) and German mustard or slice and serve on toasted rye bread with Emmental and mayonnaise.

Makes about 800–900g

For the spiced brine

200g salt

100g caster sugar

4 bay leaves

4 cloves

2 star anise

1 cinnamon or cassia stick

5–6 juniper berries

20 black peppercorns

4 blades mace

Small bunch fresh thyme

10g saltpetre (available
 from specialist suppliers
 – optional)

2 litres water

1kg piece brisket, rolled
 and tied (ask your
 butcher)

2 large onions, cut into
 eighths

4 bay leaves

1 tbsp black peppercorns

Put all the ingredients for the brine into a large pan and bring to the boil, stirring occasionally to help the salt and sugar dissolve. Remove from the heat and allow to cool.

Place the beef into a large plastic container and pour over the brine water along with all of the spices. Make sure that the meat is completely submerged in the brine – you may have to weight it down. Alternatively, use a thick zip seal bag and squeeze out as much air as possible before sealing.

Now for the hard part… the waiting! You will need to leave your beef in the fridge for 10 days, turning it over every day. Trust me, it will be worth it!

After 10 days take the meat out of the brine, pat dry with kitchen paper and place in a large pan with the onions, bay leaves and peppercorns. Add enough cold water to cover and then simmer, covered on a low heat, for 3–4 hours, making sure that the pan is always topped up with water. The meat should be completely tender.

Remove from the water and, when cool enough to handle, slice and serve. The salt beef will keep in the fridge for up to a week.

CHEAT'S MOUSSAKA

Moussaka is probably the most famous of all Greek dishes. My simplified version has a yoghurt-based topping instead of the traditional white sauce, making it perfect for a quick, mid-week supper. It's also a fantastic example of a dish that uses only one spice, cinnamon, which really comes into its own when used in savoury dishes.

Serves 4

7 tbsp light olive oil

1 large onion, finely
  chopped

2 cloves garlic, finely
  chopped

500g lamb mince

400g tin chopped tomatoes

2 tbsp tomato purée

2 tsp ground cinnamon

1 tbsp finely chopped
  fresh oregano

500ml lamb stock

2 large aubergines, sliced
  into 5mm rounds

Salt and freshly ground
  black pepper

For the topping

250g Greek yoghurt

2 eggs

2 egg yolks

150g mature Cheddar
  cheese, grated

Salt and freshly ground
  black pepper

Preheat the oven to 180°C/350°F/Gas mark 4.

Heat 2 tablespoons of the oil in a large pan and fry the onion over a medium heat until soft and starting to colour. Add the garlic and cook for another 2 minutes.

Add the mince to the pan and cook for 10–12 minutes until nicely browned. Add the tomatoes, tomato purée cinnamon, oregano and stock and cook, partially covered, for about 1 hour, stirring every 10 minutes or so to prevent it sticking.

While the meat is cooking, heat the remaining olive oil in a pan and fry the aubergine slices over a medium heat for 4–5 minutes, until golden but not crisp. Drain on kitchen paper, season with salt and pepper and set aside.

To assemble, spoon one-third of the lamb mixture into the bottom of an ovenproof dish and top with a layer of aubergine slices. Add another layer of meat, then a layer of aubergine and repeat until all the meat and aubergine slices have been used up.

Whisk together the ingredients for the topping and pour this mixture over the top. Cook in the oven for 30–40 minutes, until the top is golden.

BEEF RENDANG

Rendang is a classic Malaysian curry that should be rich and robust, yet delicate enough for the spices to shine through. It also uses a cheap cut of beef – shin or cheek – cooked long and slow so the meat softens beautifully. The spice mix is quite labour-intensive so it is a good idea to make up a large batch and freeze it, defrosting it as and when you need it. If you can, make this the day before you are going to eat it, to let those flavours develop.

Serves 4

For the spice mix
1 lemongrass stalk, outer
  layer removed and
  roughly chopped
2 red chillies, chopped
2 tbsp coriander seeds
1 tsp cumin seeds
1 tsp ground turmeric
5 tbsp vegetable oil
2 onions, finely sliced
4 cloves garlic, crushed
5cm piece fresh galangal,
  peeled and finely grated
  (use ginger if you can't
  find galangal)
5 green cardamom pods
2 star anise
4 cloves
2 cinnamon sticks
2 bay leaves

1kg beef shin or cheek, cut
  into 4–5cm cubes
400ml coconut milk
500ml hot beef stock

Crush the lemongrass and red chillies together in a pestle and mortar or whizz in a small food processor or spice grinder and set aside.

Grind the coriander and cumin seeds together in a spice grinder or with a pestle and mortar. Mix in the turmeric and set aside.

Heat the oil in a large pan over a medium heat, then add the onions, garlic, galangal or ginger and lemongrass and chilli mixture. Cook gently for 15 minutes or until the onions have softened and are starting to brown at the edges. Tie the cardamom pods, star anise and cloves in a piece of muslin and add to the pan along with the cinnamon sticks, ground spices and bay leaves. Cook for another 1–5 minutes, taking care not to let the mixture stick or burn.

Add the cubed beef and brown on all sides. Stir for a few minutes until the meat is completely coated with the spice mixture. Add the coconut milk, bring to the boil, and then add the hot stock.

Reduce the heat, cover and leave to simmer for at least 2 hours, stirring occasionally. Take off the lid and simmer for a further 30–40 minutes. You should end up with a thick, almost dry mixture. Remove the cinnamon sticks, bay leaves and muslin pouch with the whole spices and discard.

Serve with steamed basmati rice.

TERIYAKI-GLAZED SIRLOIN

There is something so utterly satisfying about teriyaki – sweet, salty and laden with umami. It's as delicate as it is powerful and works beautifully with fish or with a robust piece of sirloin as in this recipe.

Serves 4

For the teriyaki glaze
500ml beef stock
1 star anise
1 tsp Sichuan peppercorns
4 tbsp dark brown sugar
5 tbsp mirin
5 tbsp sake
5 tbsp dark soy sauce

500g sirloin, in one piece
2 tbsp vegetable oil
1 tsp sea salt
2 spring onions, very
  thinly sliced
4 tsp sesame seeds

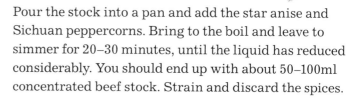

Preheat the oven to 200°C/400°F/Gas mark 6.

Pour the stock into a pan and add the star anise and Sichuan peppercorns. Bring to the boil and leave to simmer for 20–30 minutes, until the liquid has reduced considerably. You should end up with about 50–100ml concentrated beef stock. Strain and discard the spices.

Mix the stock with the remaining glaze ingredients and bring to the boil. Allow to simmer for 10 minutes and then remove from the heat.

Place a griddle or frying pan over a high heat until it is smoking hot. Meanwhile rub the sirloin with the vegetable oil and season with sea salt. When the pan is really hot, place the beef, fat side down, in the pan and leave for 2–3 minutes. Turn and sear for 2 minutes on all other sides.

Place the beef in a roasting tin and cook in the oven for 12–15 minutes, then remove and allow to rest. After 15 minutes, add the resting juices to the teriyaki glaze.

Slice the beef into thin slices, arrange on a plate and pour over the teriyaki glaze. Scatter over the sliced spring onions and sesame seeds and serve.

BEEF FILLET WITH FENUGREEK & POTATO CRUST

This is my take on classic steak and chips, but with the unexpected grassy flavour of fenugreek leaves. The potatoes are cut into tiny cubes and deep-fried to create a gorgeous crust for the beef fillet. Serve the remaining potatoes in little bowls alongside the beef.

Serves 4

2 large floury potatoes
  (Maris Piper), peeled
800g beef fillet (as uniform
  a piece as possible)
2 tbsp light olive oil
Oil, for deep-frying
2 tsp dried fenugreek
  leaves, finely crumbled
1 tsp Dijon mustard
Salt and freshly ground
  black pepper

Preheat the oven to 200°C/400°F/Gas mark 6.

Cut the potatoes into very thin slices, about 1–2mm thick (this is easiest using a mandoline). Cut these slices into 1-2mm thick matchsticks, then turn and cut again into 1-2mm dice. Put the potatoes in a sieve and rinse thoroughly in cold water to remove any excess starch, then dry on a clean tea towel.

Rub the beef fillet with the olive oil and season with salt and pepper. Heat a frying pan until very hot and sear the beef for just 1 minute on each side or until browned all over. Transfer to a roasting tin and cook in the oven for 18–20 minutes (for medium rare). Remove from the oven and transfer to a plate to rest for at least 10–15 minutes.

Meanwhile, pour the oil for deep-frying into a large, heavy-bottomed pan to a depth of 5cm and heat to about 180°C/350°F (a cube of bread should sizzle and turn golden in about 30 seconds). Deep-fry the potatoes, stirring gently, for 3–4 minutes. When they start to turn golden you need to get them out of the oil quickly; I find the easiest and quickest way to do this is to place a sieve over another large pan and then pour the potatoes and hot oil through the sieve. Take care to avoid any splashes of hot oil.

Leave the potatoes to drain in the sieve then spread out in a roasting tin. Add the dried fenugreek leaves and season with salt and pepper.

Smear the beef with the mustard and then roll in the potatoes until it is all covered. You can either roll the whole fillet as one piece or cut the beef into four portions and roll them individually. Serve immediately.

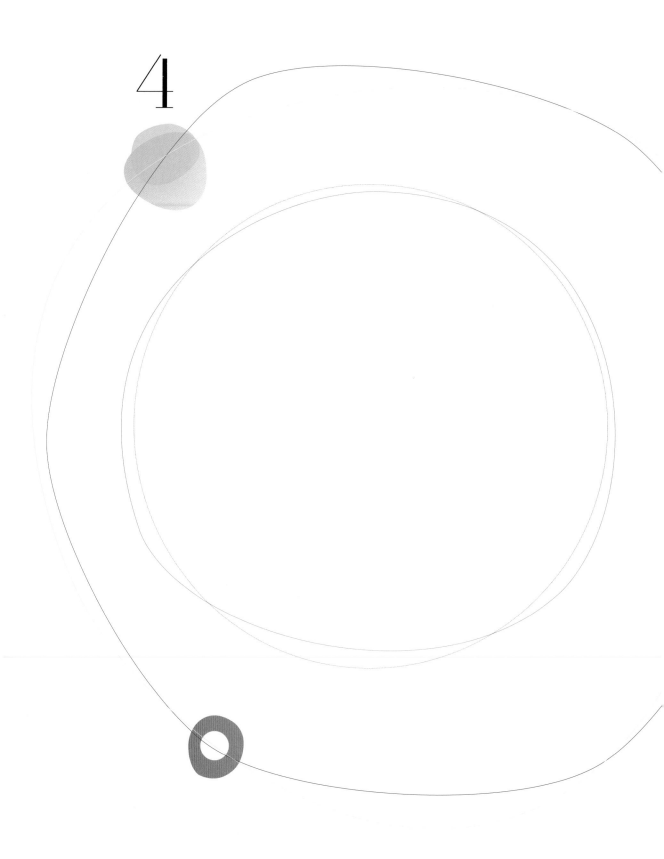

4

CHICKEN

& OTHER BIRDS

SUPER SIMPLE CHICKEN CURRY

My mother taught me how to make this dish when I was 11 years old and it was the first time I ever cooked with spices. I have cooked it countless times over the years; it's a fantastic starting point if you have never made curry and the chicken can be replaced with lamb, fish or vegetables. The way the spices are used here is the basis for innumerable dishes: simply fry whole spices to release their aroma, add onion, ginger and garlic and then add ground spices, followed by the meat of your choice and some stock.

Serves 4

2 tbsp vegetable oil

6 cloves

4 green cardamom pods

1 cinnamon stick

2 onions, finely chopped

4 cloves garlic, very finely
  chopped

4cm piece fresh ginger,
  peeled and very finely
  grated

1 tsp ground turmeric

4 tsp ground coriander

2 tsp ground cumin

½ tsp red chilli powder

75ml water

250g fresh tomatoes,
  whizzed in a blender

1 whole chicken, jointed
  into 8 pieces, or
  8 chicken thighs

250ml chicken stock

4 tbsp roughly chopped
  fresh coriander

Salt and freshly ground
  black pepper

Heat the oil in a large, lidded pan and, when hot, add the cloves, cardamom pods and cinnamon stick. Fry for about 3–4 minutes over a medium heat.

Add the onions and fry for 10–15 minutes, until golden. Add the garlic and ginger and cook for a further 2 minutes. Stir in the ground spices and cook for 2 minutes then pour in the water and cook for another 5 minutes, stirring constantly.

Add the blended tomatoes and cook for 10 minutes before adding the chicken pieces. Cover and cook for 5 minutes, then add the stock and cook, covered, for 10 minutes. Remove the lid, increase the heat and cook for a further 10 minutes until the chicken is cooked through and the sauce has started to thicken up.

Season to taste and sprinkle over the chopped coriander. Serve with steamed rice, naan bread and Cucumber Raita (see page 206) or Kachumber (see page 204).

SHERRY BRAISED CHICKEN LIVERS WITH ALMONDS AND PAPRIKA

Chicken livers are often neglected in home cooking but they are inexpensive and tasty, easily cooked in no time at all. The combination of sherry, almonds and smoky paprika is one I associate strongly with Spanish cooking.

Serves 4

2 tbsp light olive oil

1 banana shallot or 2
  shallots, finely diced

1 sprig fresh thyme

2 cloves garlic, finely sliced

500g chicken livers,
  trimmed

60ml sherry (I use Palo
  Cortado or Oloroso)

1 tbsp sherry vinegar

¼ tsp smoked paprika

2 tbsp flaked almonds

3 tbsp roughly chopped
  flat-leaf parsley

Salt and freshly ground
  black pepper

Juice of ½ lemon

Toasted brioche or
  sourdough bread,
  to serve

Heat the oil in a pan and fry the shallots for about 5 minutes until they start to soften. Add the thyme and garlic and cook for another 2 minutes.

Increase the heat, add the livers and sear on all sides. Add the sherry and sherry vinegar – stand back, as the liquid may catch light in the pan. Reduce the heat and add the paprika, almonds and parsley and stir for a couple of minutes.

Season to taste, squeeze over a little lemon juice and serve on toasted brioche or sourdough.

CHICKEN LAKSA

A good chicken laksa is hard to beat. Fiery hot and layered with flavours, this is one moreish dish. The creaminess that comes from the coconut milk helps keep the chilli heat at bay while the turmeric gives the dish its trademark golden colour and the spices add a warming, delicate layering of flavours. You will only need half the spice paste for this dish but it's always a good idea to make a larger batch as you can freeze it or keep in the fridge for up to two weeks.

Serves 4

For the laksa paste

2 shallots, roughly chopped

3 cloves garlic

2 red chillies

5cm piece fresh ginger, peeled and chopped

3 tsp chopped fresh coriander (leaves and stalks)

Zest and juice of 1 lime

1 lemongrass stalk, outer layer removed and roughly chopped

2 tbsp fish sauce

2 tsp ground coriander

1 tsp ground turmeric

50ml vegetable oil

1 litre chicken stock

2 chicken breasts, skinned

200g raw prawns, peeled

400ml coconut milk

100g beansprouts

100g cooked rice noodles

2 hard-boiled eggs, quartered

1 red chilli, very finely sliced

2 tbsp roughly chopped fresh mint

2 tbsp roughly chopped fresh coriander

2 limes, cut into wedges

Salt

Start by making the laksa paste. Blend all the ingredients in a food processor until you have a smooth paste. Heat the oil in a frying pan over a medium heat and fry the paste for 5–7 minutes until you can see that the oil has separated from the paste.

Spoon the laksa paste into a large pan and place over a medium heat. As soon as the paste starts sizzling, add the stock and bring to the boil.

Once the stock comes to a simmer, add the chicken and cook for 15 minutes, then add the prawns and cook for a further 3 minutes.

Stir through the coconut milk and return to the boil. Add the beansprouts and cooked noodles.

Remove the chicken breasts from the pan and slice thickly. Return to the pan with the egg quarters and stir gently to heat through. Season to taste and serve topped with the sliced chilli, mint and coriander and wedges of lime.

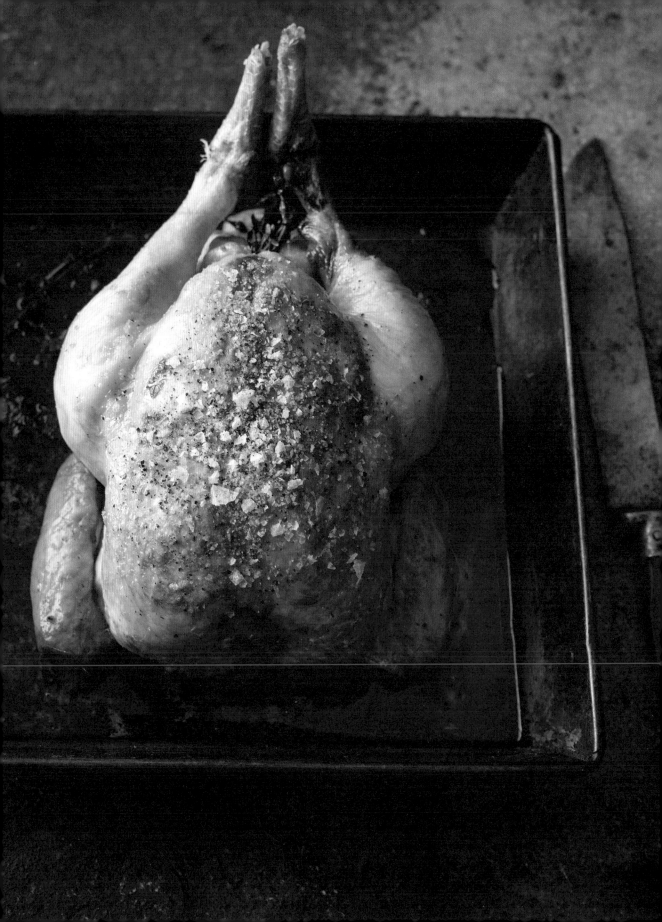

ROAST CHICKEN WITH GARLIC & PAPRIKA

One of the first things that I think of when I hear the words comfort food has to be roast chicken, mashed potatoes and gravy. At its best, it is hard to beat and with a few aromatic herbs and a dash of smoky paprika added, the roast chicken is elevated to something otherworldly. Spanish flavours work in perfect harmony with chicken, especially served with buttered greens and Vanilla Mash (see page 133).

Serves 4

1 large free-range chicken,
  about 1.5kg
1 whole garlic bulb, sliced
  in half horizontally
3 sprigs fresh thyme
2 tsp light olive oil
1 lemon
Salt and freshly ground
  black pepper

For the spiced butter
25g softened unsalted
  butter
1½ tsp fennel seeds
½ tsp smoked Spanish
  paprika
2 sprigs fresh thyme,
  leaves picked
Salt and freshly ground
  black pepper

Preheat the oven to 220°C/400°F/Gas mark 6.

Place the butter in a bowl and mix in the fennel seeds, paprika, thyme leaves and salt and pepper until you have a smooth, soft mixture.

Starting at the neck end of the chicken, slide your fingers under the skin of the breast to loosen it (try not to tear the skin). Spread the spiced butter under the skin using your fingers then massage from the outside to spread it evenly under the skin.

Place the garlic and thyme in the cavity of the chicken and then brush the top of the chicken with oil and season with salt and pepper. Place in a roasting tin and roast in the oven for 15 minutes, then turn the temperature down to 180°C/350°F/Gas mark 4. Continue to roast in the oven for 20 minutes per 500g, plus 20 minutes (so a 1.5kg bird would take 1 hour and 20 minutes) or until cooked through. To test, remove from the oven and pierce the thickest part of the thigh with a skewer – the juices should run clear.

Leave to rest in a warm place for about 15 minutes before serving with a squeeze of the lemon over the top.

CHICKEN HAINAN

A one-pot wonder that is extremely straightforward. Originally from China, there are now infinite versions of this recipe all over South East Asia. The garnishes may seem a bit of work but trust me, the flavour notes and texture they add are worth it.

Serves 4–6

1 large free-range chicken,
    about 1.5kg
3 litres chicken stock
12 spring onions, trimmed
    but left whole
3 cloves garlic
4 x 1cm slices fresh ginger
2 star anise
1 tbsp black peppercorns
1 cinnamon or cassia stick
Small bunch fresh
    coriander, finely chopped,
    stalks removed
    and reserved
150ml vegetable oil
1 large onion, finely sliced
50ml dark soy sauce
50ml white vinegar
2 green finger chillies,
    very finely chopped
2 ripe tomatoes, finely
    sliced
½ cucumber, very finely
    sliced
2 tbsp sesame oil
Steamed rice, to serve
Salt

Remove any trussing string from the chicken and place it into a pan that is large enough to hold it comfortably. Pour in the stock and add the spring onions, garlic, ginger, star anise, peppercorns, cinnamon or cassia and the stalks from the fresh coriander.

Place over a medium to high heat and bring to the boil. Reduce the heat, cover and simmer for 30–35 minutes.

Meanwhile heat the vegetable oil in a pan and fry the sliced onion over a medium heat until golden brown, about 30 minutes. Drain on kitchen paper and set aside.

Remove the chicken from the stock, transfer to a plate and leave to rest. Return the pan to the heat and boil the stock for 15 minutes, until it has reduced by about one-third.

While the stock is reducing, prepare all your garnishes. Mix together the soy sauce, white vinegar and chopped chillies in a small bowl. Put the chopped coriander leaves, fried onions, tomatoes and cucumber in separate small bowls.

Brush the chicken with the sesame oil, season lightly with salt and then carve. I usually take the breasts off first and slice them and then shred the legs and thighs with two forks.

Now it's just an assembly job. Take a bowl with some rice, pour over some of the reduced stock, add a few slices of the chicken and then top with coriander and each of the garnishes.

CHICKEN CHUKKA

This recipe has taken me years to perfect. I first tasted chicken chukka at the tiny and unassuming restaurant Dosa n Chutny in Tooting and soon became a regular there. This is my own version; the nuttiness of the coconut together with aromatic curry leaves, spices and the kick of chilli give this chicken dish a real depth.

Serves 4

50g desiccated coconut

2 cinnamon or cassia sticks

2 star anise

2 whole dried red chillies

1 tsp black peppercorns

2 tsp fennel seeds

2 tsp ground coriander

½ tsp hot chilli powder

75–100ml water

1 tsp ground turmeric

½ tsp salt

4 tbsp vegetable oil

2 red onions, finely chopped

2 tsp garlic and ginger paste (see page 215)

3 tbsp fresh curry leaves

150g tomatoes, roughly chopped

500g boneless and skinless chicken, cut into 3–4cm pieces (use a mixture of breast and thigh)

2 tbsp finely chopped fresh coriander

Juice of ½ lemon

Toast the coconut in a dry frying pan over a low to medium heat, stirring every minute or so until it turns golden brown. You have to watch the coconut like a hawk as it can burn quickly and if this happens you will have to start again as burnt coconut tastes very bitter.

Tip the toasted coconut onto a plate. Into the same pan add the cinnamon or cassia sticks, star anise, dried chillies, peppercorns and fennel seeds. Roast in the pan for about 5 minutes until you can smell those fabulous aromas, then add the ground coriander and chilli powder and stir for 2–3 minutes. Add enough water to form a paste and cook for another minute or two.

Remove the cinnamon sticks and whole chillies and set aside. Add the toasted coconut, turmeric and salt to the pan. Grind to a thick paste, using either a spice grinder or a pestle and mortar. Set aside.

Heat the oil in a pan over a low heat and slowly cook the onions until they are soft and starting to colour slightly, about 10–12 minutes. Add the garlic and ginger paste, increase the heat and stir-fry for 2–3 minutes. Add the curry leaves and stir for a minute before adding the tomatoes and then the spice paste. Return the cinnamon or cassia sticks, star anise and whole chillies to the pan and cook for about 5 minutes, stirring continuously until the tomatoes start to break up.

Add the chicken pieces and cook, covered, for 10 minutes. Remove the lid and cook for a further 5 minutes until the chicken is cooked through.

Stir through the fresh coriander and lemon juice, discard the cinnamon or cassia sticks and serve alongside steamed rice or piping hot buttered naan.

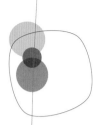

MOLE IN MEXICO

I was very young when my family lived in Mexico but I will always remember the taste of Mole Poblano. A beautiful, glossy, rich, deep brown sauce, which is a cornerstone of Mexican cooking. It is cooked with turkey, chicken or pork and consists of a complex blend of spices and chillies, such as ancho, mulato, pasilla and chipotle, with richness coming from the addition of dark chocolate.

One Sunday afternoon my family and I were at a friend's house for lunch and I had disappeared, causing a small degree of panic amongst the adults (a trick which I mastered by the age of three, when I vanished during a trip to Teotihuacan and was found attempting to climb the Temple of the Moon) who frantically started a search for me. I was found, sitting cross-legged and chattering in Spanish to the elderly gardener who had shared his lunch of Mole Poblano with me. The memory of that flavour – deep, rich, hot with chilli and heady with cinnamon and coriander – will never leave me. Mole is a dish I go back to time and time again.

TURKEY MOLE

This is my simplified version of that mole I tasted many years ago, which is a great deal easier, but just as tasty!

Serves 6

3 tbsp vegetable oil

750g turkey breast, cut into large chunks

2 large onions, chopped

3 cloves garlic, chopped

1 tbsp chilli powder

2 tsp ground cumin

2 tsp ground coriander

3 cinnamon sticks

2 tbsp malt vinegar

4 tbsp tomato purée

2 chipotle chillies, chopped or 1 tbsp chipotle paste

2 litres chicken stock

3 tbsp smooth peanut butter

75g dark chocolate

2 tbsp sesame seeds

Rice or flour tortillas, to serve

Guacamole (see page 205), to serve

Preheat the oven to 180°C/350°F/Gas mark 4.

Heat the oil in large, ovenproof pan over a medium heat and when hot, add the turkey. Cook until browned all over. Remove and set aside.

In the same pan, fry the onions for about 5–10 minutes, until soft. Then add the garlic, ground spices and cinnamon sticks. Cook for 5 minutes.

Add the vinegar and tomato purée and cook for another 2–3 minutes. Add the chipotle chillies or paste, stock, peanut butter and chocolate and stir until smooth. Cook, uncovered, for about 15 minutes and then return the turkey to the pan. Cover with foil or a lid and cook in the oven for 45 minutes.

Remove the turkey from the pan and set aside on a serving dish. Pass the sauce through a sieve into a small pan and place over a medium heat. Cook until thick and dark, about 10–15 minutes.

Pour the sauce over the turkey and scatter with sesame seeds. Serve with rice or in tortillas with a side of guacamole.

DUCK BRAISED WITH STAR ANISE, SOY & GALANGAL

This is a stunning centrepiece dish with a difference. It looks, smells and tastes amazing! It's inspired by the cuisines of Malaysia and Indonesia – the trademark ingredients of galangal, kecap manis and star anise pinpointing its geographical roots. I think it needs nothing more to accompany it than steamed rice and some greens wilted with a little garlic and sesame oil.

Serves 4

3 tbsp caster sugar

5 slices galangal, about the thickness of a pound coin

3 cloves garlic

500ml chicken stock

1 tbsp rice vinegar

5 tbsp kecap manis (alternatively use dark soy sauce with a pinch of sugar)

3 star anise

1 whole Gressingham duck

2 tsp Chinese five-spice powder

1 tsp salt

Bunch spring onions, very finely sliced

Plum and Black Cardamom Sauce (see page 208), to serve (optional)

Place a wok over a high heat and add the sugar. As it starts to caramelise and turn thick and sticky add the galangal and garlic. Add 100ml of the stock – the sugar will solidify instantly. Keep the wok on the heat; once the sugar has melted again add the rest of the stock, the rice vinegar, kecap manis (or soy sauce) and star anise and stir until smooth.

Rub the duck all over, inside and out, with the five-spice powder and salt.

Add the duck to the wok and baste with the liquid. Reduce the heat to very low and cook, covered, for 1½–2 hours, basting the duck thoroughly every 10 minutes or so. If it looks like the pan is going to run dry, add another 200ml water.

Remove the lid for the last 15 minutes of the cooking time and increase the heat to make the remaining cooking sauce thick and glossy.

You can also make this in a lidded casserole dish and cook it in the oven. Preheat the oven to 140°C/275°F/Gas mark 1 and follow the method as above until you add the duck. Cook in the oven for 1½–2 hours, basting as before. Cook uncovered for the last 15 minutes and take care not to let the liquid dry out.

Carve the duck and arrange on a serving dish. Spoon the sauce over and scatter with the sliced spring onions. This dish is also wonderful with Plum and Cardamom Black sauce.

SPICED CONFIT DUCK WITH PISTACHIO NUTS

This is the perfect example of how spices can bring new dimensions to traditional recipes and techniques. The duck legs are infused with the flavours of the whole spices without being overpowered and the leftover spiced duck fat is fantastic for cooking roast potatoes – just keep it in a jar in the fridge. I love sweet and sharp sauces with game – try this on some toasted sourdough with Plum and Black Cardamom Sauce and a few cornichons. Perfect for picnics!

Serves 6 as a starter

4 duck legs
250ml duck or goose fat
100ml white wine
2 star anise
8 juniper berries
1 cinnamon stick
1 tsp black peppercorns
2 blades mace
8 cloves
2 bay leaves
2 cloves garlic
2 sprigs fresh thyme
Large pinch sea salt
Small bunch flat-leaf
    parsley, finely chopped
50g shelled and roasted
    pistachios, skins
    rubbed off
1 lemon
Toasted sourdough and
    cornichons, to serve
Plum and Black
    Cardamom
    Sauce (see page 208),
    to serve

Preheat the oven to 140°C/275°F/Gas mark 1.

Place the duck legs in a deep roasting tin and add all the ingredients except the parsley, pistachios and lemon juice. Cover tightly with foil and place in the oven for 3–4 hours, until the meat is falling off the bone.

Carefully lift the legs out of the tray and shred with two forks, discarding the skin, bones and sinew. Put the shredded meat into a bowl. Pour the cooking fat through a sieve and set aside.

Pour just under half the flavoured duck fat over your shredded duck, then add the parsley, pistachios and a squeeze of lemon juice and mix thoroughly. It should be lovely and moist so add more of the duck fat if you feel it needs it.

Spoon into individual ramekins or a large Kilner jar and chill in the fridge for a couple of hours. Serve on toasted sourdough with cornichons and Plum and Black Cardamom Sauce.

ACHARI SPICED DUCK

I spent ages working on this dish; I knew exactly what I wanted it to taste like and was determined to get it right – the first attempt actually made my wife cry it was so bad! I am delighted to say that it is now one of her favourite dishes. It is the complexity of the flavour that really stands out; there are a lot of ingredients but when all working together you end up with a beautiful, elegant and delicious dish.

Serves 4

3 tbsp vegetable oil

2 whole dried red chillies

3 cloves garlic, crushed

5cm piece ginger, peeled
   and grated

½ tsp red chilli powder

½ tsp garam masala

1 tsp ground turmeric

Pinch asafoetida

1 tsp sea salt

2 Gressingham duck leg
   joints, roughly chopped
   (including bones)

250ml chicken stock

4 Gressingham duck
   breasts

1 tbsp unsalted butter

3 tbsp roughly chopped
   fresh coriander

Plum and Black
   Cardamom
   Sauce (see page 208),
   to serve

For the achari spice mix

2 tsp fennel seeds

½ tsp nigella seeds

½ tsp brown mustard seeds

½ tsp fenugreek seeds

Preheat the oven to 180°C/350°F/Gas mark 4.

Coarsley grind the ingredients for the spice mix using either a pestle and mortar or a spice grinder. Set aside.

Heat the oil in a frying pan and add the dried chillies. After 1 minute add the garlic and ginger and fry for a further minute.

Add the achari spice mix and after a minute add the chilli powder, garam masala, turmeric, asafoetida and sea salt. Add the chopped duck and cook for 2–3 minutes. Add the stock and cook for 20 minutes, stirring occasionally. Strain the contents of the pan, discarding the bones, and keep the sauce to one side.

Meanwhile place a separate frying pan over a low heat and add the duck breasts, skin-side down. After 10–12 minutes the skin should be nicely browned; turn the breasts over and add the butter to the pan along with half of the reserved sauce. Place the pan in the oven for 8–10 minutes.

Slice the duck, sprinkle with the chopped coriander and serve with the rest of the duck sauce and some Plum and Black Cardamom Sauce.

CHENNAI SPICED GUINEA FOWL

The key to this dish is the Chennai masala paste, which is bursting with ingredients and intricate flavours. Once you have made the paste the rest is plain sailing so I have suggested making a decent quantity so you can freeze the remainder for next time. This way you can make this dish in practically no time next time. Use the paste again as a base for a curry; just fry a couple of tablespoons of the spice paste in a little vegetable oil, add chicken pieces and some stock and simmer until cooked.

Serves 4

4 guinea fowl breasts,
  skin on
300g unsalted butter
Salt and freshly ground
  black pepper

*For the Chennai
  masala paste*
8 tbsp desiccated coconut
1 tsp coriander seeds
½ tsp fennel seeds
1 dried red chilli
½ black peppercorns
1 cinnamon stick, broken
  into pieces
2 cloves
20 fresh curry leaves
1 tsp ground turmeric
5 tbsp vegetable oil
1 red onion, finely chopped
1 tsp garlic and ginger
  paste (see page 215)
2 tomatoes, finely chopped

Make the Chennai masala paste by toasting the coconut in a dry frying pan until golden and you can smell that wonderful nuttiness. Drain on kitchen paper to dry off any oil and set aside.

Add the coriander seeds, fennel seeds, dried red chilli, peppercorns, cinnamon stick, cloves and curry leaves to the pan and cook for 4–5 minutes over a low heat. Add the turmeric and 2 tablespoons of the oil to the mixture and cook for 30 seconds.

Allow to cool slightly before adding the coconut and grinding the mixture to a smooth paste using a pestle and mortar or a spice grinder. You should end up with a thick and deliciously fragrant dark paste.

Heat the remaining oil in the same pan and fry the onion for about 5 minutes, then add the garlic and ginger paste and cook for another 4–5 minutes or until the mixture starts to colour. Add the tomatoes and cook for a further 5–7 minutes.

Add the spice paste to the pan and cook together for 10 minutes, stirring continuously, or until the oil separates out of the paste mixture. Allow to cool.

Mix two tablespoons of the Chennai masala paste with the butter. You can keep the remainder in the fridge in an airtight container for about a week or in the freezer for a couple of months.

Preheat the oven to 200°C/400°F/Gas mark 6.

Push the butter mixture under the skin of the guinea fowl and massage with your fingers to spread it around evenly. Season the breasts with salt and pepper and place in a roasting tin. Cook in the oven for 12–15 minutes until the skin is golden. Allow to rest for 5 minutes before serving.

BARBECUED PIGEON WITH SPICED PEA PURÉE

This works beautifully on a barbecue as the pigeon takes on an irresistible smokiness. You can buy pigeon at some large supermarkets but any good butcher should be able to get you some. Alternatively you could use duck breasts instead of pigeon.

Serves 4

4 pigeon crowns
  (on the bone)
1 lime, quartered
Salt

For the marinade
2 tbsp garlic and ginger
  paste (see page 215)
Juice of 1 lemon
Juice of 1 lime
2 tsp vegetable oil
½ tsp coarsely ground
  black pepper
½ tsp salt

For the pea purée
1 tbsp vegetable oil
1 onion, finely chopped
3 sprigs fresh curry leaves
1 tsp brown mustard seeds
1 green finger chilli,
  seeded
  and chopped
250g frozen peas
100ml coconut milk or
  chicken stock
4 tbsp roughly chopped
  fresh coriander
2 tbsp roughly chopped
  fresh mint

Mix all the marinade ingredients together in a large bowl. Add the pigeon crown and turn to coat in the marinade. Place in the fridge for at least 1 hour or overnight if possible.

To make the pea purée, heat the oil in a frying pan and add the onion. Fry for about 10 minutes until soft and starting to colour. Add the curry leaves, mustard seeds and chilli and fry for another 5 minutes. Add the peas and the coconut milk or stock and bring to the boil.

Remove from the heat and tip the pea mixture into a blender with the coriander and mint and blend until smooth. Set aside until ready to serve. If you are making this in advance then reheat gently before serving with the pigeon.

To cook the pigeon on a barbecue, place over hot coals and cook for 3 minutes each side. Allow to rest for 5–10 minutes. Alternatively, pan-fry for 3–5 minutes each side and rest as before.

To serve, take the breast fillets off the joint and then cut each breast into four or five slices (the meat should be pink in the middle) and arrange on top of the pea purée. Finish with a squeeze of lime and a pinch of salt.

TANDOORI POUSSIN

Although this would traditionally be cooked in a tandoor oven, these delicate little birds are just as tasty cooked under the grill or on a barbecue. The yoghurt binds all the spices together and helps tenderise the poussin, giving you meat that just falls off the bone. You will need to allow two days for marinating but other than that it is as simple a recipe as you could wish for.

Serves 4

4 poussins, spatchcocked
　(ask your butcher to do
　this for you)
2 limes, halved
Naan bread, to serve
Kachumber (see page 204)
　or sliced red onions,
　to serve

For the first marinade
2 tbsp garlic and ginger
　paste (see page 215)
Juice of 1 lime
½ tsp chilli powder
½ tsp ground turmeric
¼ tsp ground white pepper
4 tbsp vegetable oil
¼ tsp salt

For the second marinade
½ tsp paprika
½ tsp fennel seeds
½ tsp ground cumin
½ tsp ground coriander
¼ tsp garam masala
250g Greek yoghurt
Juice of 1 lemon
Salt and freshly ground
　black pepper

Mix together all the ingredients for the first marinade and rub all over the poussins. Cover and leave in the fridge for a few hours or overnight if possible.

Mix together all the ingredients for the second marinade and repeat the process; smear all over the poussins and leave to marinade for another couple of hours or overnight, if possible.

To grill, lay the poussins on a rack and cook under a preheated grill on medium to high for about 20 minutes, turning every 5 minutes. Increase the heat to high and cook skin-side up for a further 5 minutes.

Alternatively, if cooking on a barbecue, preheat the oven to 200°C/400°F/Gas mark 6. Put the poussins in a roasting tin and cook in the oven for 10 minutes. Finish off on the barbecue for a final 5–10 minutes, turning them regularly so that they don't burn.

Squeeze over the limes and serve with warm naan bread and Kachumber or sliced red onions.

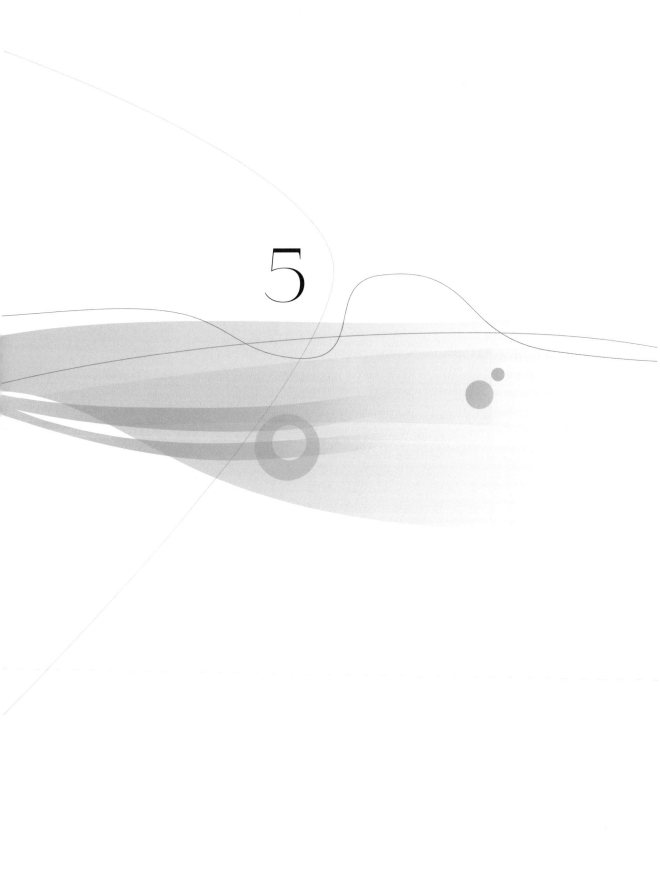

5

VEGETABLES

& GRAINS

SAFFRON POMMES ANNA

I've given this classic French dish an extra dimension by adding saffron, although I cannot stress enough to use the saffron sparingly – too much and it will overpower the dish and become unpleasant. This would usually be a side dish but I think it makes a pretty decent meal in itself served with a salad and a glass of chilled white wine.

Serves 4–6

500g floury potatoes (Maris Piper or King Edward)
100g unsalted butter
7–8 strands saffron, soaked in 2 tsp warm water
Vegetable oil, for greasing
Salt and freshly ground black pepper

Preheat the oven to 180°C/350°F/Gas mark 4. Peel the potatoes and slice as thinly as possible using a sharp knife or a mandoline.

Melt the butter in a large pan and add the saffron strands and soaking liquid, along with some salt and pepper. Tip the sliced potatoes into the pan and stir through the butter so that each slice is coated.

Lightly oil a small, ovenproof frying pan and place over a low heat. Neatly layer the bottom of the pan with overlapping slices of potato; repeat until you have used up all the potatoes.

Cover with foil, place into the oven and cook for 1½ hours. Carefully flip the potatoes over onto a board. Cut into wedges and serve.

CAULIFLOWER CHEESE WITH A CUMIN & MACADAMIA CRUST

I may be accused of gilding the lily here, as cauliflower cheese is already a wonderful dish. The soured cream gives an extra richness and the macadamia nuts add a lovely texture to the topping, while the cumin seeds prevent the dish from becoming too sweet.

Serves 4

1 head cauliflower, cut into florets
750ml whole milk
½ onion, studded with 6 cloves
2 bay leaves
1 tsp black peppercorns
50g unsalted butter
1 tsp cumin seeds
50g plain flour
75g grated Cheddar cheese
100ml soured cream
Oil, for greasing
25g panko breadcrumbs
25g macadamia nuts whizzed in a food processor or chopped with a knife
Salt and freshly ground black pepper

Preheat the oven to 200°C/400°F/Gas mark 6.

Bring a large pan of salted water to the boil, add the cauliflower florets and cook for 5 minutes. Drain well and set aside in the colander to drain off any excess water.

Pour the milk into a pan and add the clove-studded onion, bay leaves and peppercorns. Heat gently until it just comes to a simmer and then remove from the heat. Cover and allow to sit for 10 minutes then strain the milk into a jug, discarding the onion, bay leaves and peppercorns.

Melt the butter in a separate pan; when foaming add the cumin seeds and fry for 1 minute and then add the flour, stirring continuously. When the mixture takes on a golden colour, gradually add the warm milk. Once you have a smooth paste you can add the milk more quickly. If the mixture is a bit thick add some more milk. You may find a whisk easier than a wooden spoon. Stir in 50g of the cheese and the soured cream. Season to taste.

Place the cauliflower florets into a lightly oiled ovenproof dish and pour over the cheese and cumin sauce.

Mix the breadcrumbs, macadamia nuts and remaining cheese together then sprinkle over the top of the mixture. Bake in the oven for 20 minutes, or until the top is bubbling and golden brown.

VANILLA MASH

You may wince at the thought of vanilla and potatoes together, but the addition of just a hint of vanilla really elevates this mash to new heights. Peeling the potatoes once cooked will give you the lightest, fluffiest mash possible. Serve with almost any roasted meat; it goes particularly well with Roast Chicken with Garlic and Paprika (see page 109).

Serves 4

500g floury potatoes
  (Maris Piper or King
  Edward), scrubbed
2 bay leaves
1 tbsp black peppercorns
1 vanilla pod
50g unsalted butter
250ml whole milk
Pinch sea salt

Leave the potatoes unpeeled but cut any large ones in half, so they are all roughly the same size.

Place the potatoes into a large pan of cold salted water and add the bay leaves and peppercorns. Split the vanilla pod in half lengthways and use a knife to scrape out the seeds; add both the seeds and the pod to the pan. Bring to the boil and then cook over a medium heat for 20–25 minutes, or until the potatoes are cooked through (you should be able to push a skewer through with no resistance). Strain into a jug, discarding the peppercorns, bay leaves and vanilla pod.

While the potatoes are still hot, peel them using a small sharp knife (hold the potato in a clean tea towel while you do this). Mash the potatoes in a clean pan or pass through a potato ricer into a bowl. Add the butter and milk and mix well with a spatula until you end up with deliciously smooth and creamy mash.

Season to taste with sea salt and serve immediately.

MUSHROOM PILAU

The first time I made this was for a vegetarian friend who complained that every time she went to a dinner party she was given mushroom risotto. I am pleased to report that she loved the flavours of the earthy mushrooms along with the crispy fried onions and aromatic spices – as far from an average mushroom risotto as you could imagine.

Serves 4

250g basmati rice
4 tbsp vegetable oil
6 green cardamom pods
2 cinnamon sticks
10 cloves
2 bay leaves
1 onion, thinly sliced
125g white mushrooms, sliced
2 cloves garlic, finely chopped
½ tsp salt
500ml water
Small pinch saffron
2–3 tbsp flaked almonds (optional)

Start by rinsing the rice in cold water until the water runs clear. Set aside in a sieve to allow as much water as possible to drain off.

Heat half the oil in a large pan and add the cardamom pods, cinnamon sticks, cloves and bay leaves; stir for 1 minute. Add half the sliced onion and cook for 5 minutes, then add the mushrooms and garlic and fry for another 10 minutes.

Add the rice and salt and stir until the rice is well coated in the oil. Add the water and bring to the boil.

After about 4–5 minutes much of the water will have evaporated. Stir in the saffron strands, cover and reduce the heat to the lowest possible setting. Cook for 12–15 minutes, or until the rice is tender.

Meanwhile, heat the remaining oil in a pan and fry the remaining onion slices until golden brown. Remove from the pan and drain on kitchen paper.

To serve, scatter the fried onion over the top of the pilau along with the flaked almonds, if using.

PUNJABI PARATHAS IN DELHI

When I was a child we lived in Delhi for ten amazing years. Our neighbours were a large extended Punjabi family who became very close friends. Everyone from grandparents to uncles, aunts and seemingly hordes of cousins lived in that massive house. During the holidays and weekends my brother and I spent most of our time over there – terrorising the elderly relatives and each other – and consequently ate many meals together. Theirs was fantastic, proper, home-cooked Punjabi fare and I can remember some of those flavours to this day. A particularly beautiful meal was parathas stuffed with mashed potato and chilli and laden with ghee, served with mango pickle (with an abundance of fennel seeds) and rajma – a sweetly spiced, slow-cooked dish of kidney beans. The latter is a dish I still cook regularly and you can enjoy it with almost anything. I like to serve it as part of a vegetarian meal with Cumin and Chilli Potatoes (see page 145), rice and naan, roti or paratha.

PUNJABI-STYLE KIDNEY BEANS

You should end up with a dish with delicate spicing and a sauce that is not too thick. Serve with rice and Yellow Pork (see page 70) or the Mussalam Lamb Chops (see page 81). Tell your guests to keep an eye out for the cloves and cardamom pods – they should not be eaten!

Serves 4

2 x 400g tins red kidney
  beans, drained and rinsed
3cm piece fresh ginger,
  peeled and grated
3 cloves garlic, crushed
1 green finger chilli, very
  finely chopped
500ml water
Salt and ground white
  pepper

For the spice mix
2 tbsp vegetable oil
2 tsp cumin seeds
10 cloves
2 black cardamom pods
1 large onion, finely
  chopped
3cm piece fresh ginger,
  peeled and grated
3 cloves garlic, finely sliced
1 tsp ground turmeric
1 tsp chilli powder
1 tsp ground coriander
1 tsp ground cumin
4 tomatoes, chopped
2 tbsp unsalted butter
50ml double cream
1 lime
Small bunch fresh
  coriander, roughly
  chopped
Salt

Put the kidney beans, ginger, garlic, chilli and water in a large pan and add a pinch of salt and ground white pepper. Gently bring to the boil and then reduce the heat and simmer for 15–20 minutes.

Meanwhile, in a separate non-stick pan, heat the oil and add the cumin seeds, cloves and black cardamom pods. Fry for 2–3 minutes, stirring all the time.

Add the onion and cook for 5 minutes; then add the ginger and garlic and cook for a further 2 minutes. Add the ground spices and a pinch of salt along with 3–4 tablespoons of water to prevent the spices sticking and burning. Add the chopped tomatoes and stir to form a paste. Add this to the kidney beans.

Stir in the butter, double cream and a squeeze of lime juice to taste. Cover and cook for a further 10 minutes then finish by scattering over the chopped coriander.

CHICKPEA & EGG CURRY

I love having foolproof recipes that can be made quickly using ingredients I already have in my cupboard. This is exactly one of those recipes. Chickpeas are nutritious and inexpensive and have a fantastic ability to take on any number of spices.

Serves 4

2 tbsp vegetable oil

1 large onion, finely chopped

4 tbsp tomato purée

2 tsp garlic and ginger paste (see page 215)

2 tsp ground cumin

1 tsp ground coriander

½ tsp ground turmeric

¼ tsp red chilli powder

50ml water

2 x 400g tins chickpeas, drained and rinsed

500ml vegetable or chicken stock

4 hard-boiled eggs, halved

Juice of 1 lemon

Small bunch fresh coriander, roughly chopped

Salt and freshly ground black pepper

Heat the oil in a large, lidded pan over a medium heat. When hot add the onion and fry for about 7–10 minutes until soft and starting to colour. Add the tomato purée and fry for 1 minute.

Add the garlic and ginger paste and stir for a couple of minutes, then add all the ground spices. After about 30 seconds add the water so that the spices don't stick and burn. Cook, stirring continuously, for another 2–3 minutes.

Add the chickpeas and stir until they are well coated in the spices. Pour in the stock, partially cover with the lid and cook for 15 minutes.

Remove the lid, stir well, then add the hard-boiled eggs and cook for another couple of minutes before adding the lemon juice and salt and pepper to taste. Scatter over the coriander and serve immediately.

GOAT'S CHEESE & RED ONION TART

Ever heard the phrase 'real men don't eat quiche'? Well I love quiche and I love this tart! The sharp, salty flavour of mild goat's cheese counterbalances the sweetness of the onions very well. If you want to use ready-made pastry, just roll out and sprinkle with the Parmesan and fennel seeds before folding over and rolling again.

Serves 4

200g plain flour
¼ tsp salt
1 tsp fennel seeds
2 tbsp grated Parmesan
100g cold unsalted butter, diced
2–3 tbsp ice-cold water

For the filling
2 tbsp light olive oil
500g red onions, finely sliced
1 star anise
2 sprigs fresh thyme
75ml balsamic vinegar
3 tbsp muscovado sugar
150g mild rindless goat's cheese
3 eggs
250ml double cream
Small handful chives, chopped
Pinch grated nutmeg
Salt and freshly ground black pepper

Preheat the oven to 180°C/350°F/Gas mark 4.

Mix the flour, salt, fennel seeds and Parmesan together in a large bowl and then add the butter. Using your fingertips, massage the butter into the flour until it resembles breadcrumbs. Alternatively, whizz the ingredients in a food processor.

Add the water one tablespoon at a time (you may not need all of it, just enough to hold it together). On a lightly floured surface, gently work the dough for a few seconds and form into a ball. Wrap in cling film and leave to chill in the fridge for about 25 minutes.

Meanwhile, heat the olive oil in a pan and add the onions and star anise. Fry for about 15 minutes over a medium heat until the onions are soft and golden brown in colour.

Add the thyme, balsamic vinegar and sugar and cook for a further 6–8 minutes until the mixture is thick and glossy. Set aside to cool slightly and then discard the thyme and star anise.

Roll the pastry out on a lightly floured surface until it is about the thickness of a pound coin and large enough to line a 20cm fluted tart tin. Lay the pastry in the tin and gently press it into the edges. Trim the pastry as necessary, leaving a little sticking out over the edge of the dish. Prick the bottom of the pastry all over with a fork and return to the fridge to chill for another 10–15 minutes.

Remove the pastry case from the fridge, line with non-stick baking paper and fill with either rice, dried chickpeas or baking beans. Bake in the oven for 20–25 minutes, then take out the baking paper and beans and return to the oven for a further 5–10 minutes until the pastry is pale golden.

Spread the onion mixture all over the base of the pastry case and evenly crumble over the goat's cheese. If it's too soft to crumble, mix the cheese into the egg mixture in the next stage.

Whisk together the eggs, cream, chives, nutmeg and salt and pepper. Pour into the pastry case so that it comes almost to the top and then return to the oven. Cook for 30 minutes until golden and puffed up. Allow to cool slightly before serving.

CAPONATA

Aubergines are one of my star vegetables; they are delicious as well as stunning to look at, with their deep purple lustre. Caponata is a brilliant vehicle for them and this Sicilian stew can be served hot or cold. It works well on its own with crusty bread or as an accompaniment to pork, fish or chicken. The hit of aniseed flavour from the fennel seeds really does complement the sharpness of the vinegar perfectly.

Serves 4

4 tbsp light olive oil

2 large aubergines, cut into 4cm cubes

½ tsp cumin seeds

1 tsp fennel seeds

1 red onion, finely chopped

3 cloves garlic, finely chopped

20ml red wine vinegar

100g green olives (I like to use the ones stuffed with anchovy)

4 large tomatoes, roughly chopped

Small bunch flat-leaf parsley, roughly chopped

Salt and freshly ground black pepper

Heat a large frying pan and when hot add the olive oil and the aubergines. When the aubergines have started to colour, after about 10 minutes, add the cumin and fennel seeds and cook for a further 5 minutes.

Add the onion and garlic and stir-fry for another 5 minutes. Add the vinegar and olives and stir well; cook for another 5 minutes then add the tomatoes. Leave to cook over a medium heat for 10 minutes.

Scatter over the parsley and season with salt and pepper. Serve hot or cold.

MY MEXICAN RICE

This rice dish will complement the main event but is also delicate enough not to overpower. Try it with the Turkey Mole on page 115.

Serves 4–6
200g basmati rice
4 tbsp vegetable oil
3 ripe tomatoes, whizzed in
   a blender
1 tsp chipotle paste
500ml hot chicken stock (a
   stock cube is fine)
Small bunch fresh
   coriander, finely chopped
Salt and freshly ground
   black pepper

Start by soaking the rice in cold water for 15–20 minutes, then rinse in cold water until the water runs clear. This will remove any excess starch from the rice, which can make the finished dish sticky. Leave the rice in a sieve to drain off any excess water.

Heat the oil in a lidded pan over a medium to high heat. Add the rice and stir for about 3–4 minutes until all the grains are coated in the oil and start to smell toasted.

Stir through the tomatoes and the chipotle paste, then pour in the stock and bring to the boil. Boil for 10 minutes, or until about three-quarters of the liquid has evaporated. Reduce the heat to the lowest setting, cover and leave for 20 minutes.

Remove the lid, season to taste and stir through the chopped coriander. Serve immediately.

CUMIN & CHILLI POTATOES

These crunchy cubes of potato fried with cumin seeds and chilli powder are good enough to go with almost any roasted or grilled meat – the perfect side dish for a barbecue.

Serves 4

500g floury potatoes (Maris
   Piper or King Edward),
   peeled and cut into 3cm
   cubes
3 tbsp vegetable oil
1 tsp cumin seeds
½ tsp hot chilli powder
Juice of ½ lemon
2 tbsp roughly chopped
   fresh coriander
Salt and freshly ground
   black pepper

Place the potatoes in a large pan of salted water and bring to the boil. Reduce the heat and simmer for 2 minutes, then drain. Leave in the colander to dry completely.

Heat the oil in a large frying pan and, when hot, add the cumin seeds. When they start sizzling, after about 30 seconds, add the potatoes and toss in the oil to evenly coat.

Sprinkle over the chilli powder and salt and pepper and continue to fry for about 10 minutes, turning every few minutes, until the potatoes are golden and crisp all over.

Squeeze over the lemon juice, scatter with the coriander and serve immediately.

MISO & GINGER GLAZED AUBERGINE

This is an unbelievably satisfying dish thanks to the oodles of umami from the miso. The aubergine becomes unctuous and soft and the miso and sugar combination hits every bit of your palate.

Serves 4

2 large aubergines

2–3 tbsp vegetable oil

2 tbsp brown miso paste

3 tbsp caster sugar

2 tbsp soy sauce

2 tbsp mirin

1 tsp ginger paste (see page 215)

1 clove garlic, crushed

Freshly ground black pepper

2 spring onions, very thinly sliced

Halve the aubergines lengthways and then use the tip of a very sharp knife to score a diamond pattern in the flesh of each half (make the incisions about 1cm apart).

Place the oil in a frying pan over a medium heat. Add the aubergine halves, flesh side down and cook for 6–7 minutes until golden brown. Turn them over and cook for another 5 minutes (cooking times may vary by a minute or so depending on the size of the aubergines). They should be quite soft by this point. Remove from the pan and leave to rest on some kitchen paper to get rid of any excess oil.

Preheat the grill to its highest setting. Mix together all the remaining ingredients except for the spring onions in a small bowl. Arrange the aubergine halves, flesh side up, on a grill pan and spoon the mixture over each half. Grill for 4–5 minutes until the tops are bubbling and golden.

Sprinkle over the sliced spring onions and serve immediately.

GREEN BEANS WITH COCONUT

The trinity of coconut, curry leaves and mustard seeds is one that I strongly associate with the food of southern India – the taste is irresistible. The coconut and fried curry leaves in this recipe add both flavour and texture to these crunchy green beans. Try it with Chennai Spiced Guinea Fowl (see page 122) or Monkfish with Chilli and Black Cardamom (see page 59).

Serves 4–6 as a side dish

2 tbsp vegetable oil

1 large dried red chilli

½ tsp black mustard seeds

20 fresh curry leaves

1 small red onion, finely chopped

200g green beans, topped and tailed

2 heaped tbsp desiccated coconut

Juice of ½ lemon

Salt

Heat the oil in a frying pan or wok over a medium heat and, when hot, add the chilli, mustard seeds and curry leaves. Fry until the mustard seeds start to pop, then add the onion and fry for a further 4–5 minutes, or until the onion is soft.

Add the green beans and stir well. Place a lid on the pan and cook, stirring occasionally, for about 15 minutes.

Remove the lid, increase the heat and add the coconut, lemon juice and salt to taste. Stir-fry for a couple of minutes and then serve.

CARAWAY & BALSAMIC ROASTED BEETROOT

Despite not being a huge fan of caraway seeds, I have to admit that they are essential in this dish, which I love. The earthy flavour of the beetroot works very well with the caraway and is balanced by the acidity from the balsamic vinegar. Serve warm with roast lamb and Vanilla Mash (see page 133) or leave to cool and serve as a salad.

Serves 4 as a side dish or
  2 as a salad

500g baby beetroot, peeled
  and halved, or larger
  beetroot, quartered

50ml balsamic vinegar

1 tbsp caster sugar

1 tsp caraway seeds

Zest and juice of 1 orange

50ml water

Salt and freshly ground
  black pepper

Preheat the oven to 200°C400°F/Gas mark 6.

Take a large piece of foil and fold up the sides to make a parcel. Put all of the ingredients into the centre, seal the parcel and place into a roasting tin. Cook in the oven for 1 hour – the beetroot should be just soft but still retain some bite.

Remove the beetroot from the foil parcel and carefully pour the cooking juices into a small pan. Place over a medium heat and reduce until the sauce becomes thick and glossy, about 5–10 minutes. Toss the cooked beetroot in the sauce and serve.

BLACK DAL FROM DELHI TO LONDON

One of my most enduring restaurant memories is of eating at the world-famous Bukhara restaurant in Delhi. Based at the Maurya hotel in New Delhi, this was one of the places my family went to for a real treat. My love of clay-oven cooking was kindled there as they specialised in meat dishes cooked in the tandoor. Lamb cooked for hours, the most divine tandoori chicken and enormous naan breads were some of the standout dishes for me. When Bukhara came to London as a pop-up restaurant I managed to beg, steal, borrow and cajole my way into getting one of the rare table reservations there. My expectations were sky high; many of my childhood food memories were riding on this eagerly anticipated meal. Thankfully, the food was exactly as I had remembered it – if not better – and I enjoyed every mouthful. Bukhara are probably most famous for their black dal dish – thick, rich with butter and perfectly spiced.

BLACK DAL

A well-cooked black dal is a thing of beauty… thick, creamy and utterly, utterly delicious. Served with a roti or naan this is a wonderful meal in itself – a bowl of this will rival any soup or stew. It's worth using dried beans and lentils and soaking them overnight as you get a much better texture.

Serves 4

75g kidney beans
75g urad dal
75g chana dal
1 tbsp unsalted butter
½ tsp brown mustard seeds
½ tsp cumin seeds
1 tsp ginger paste (see
  page 215)
1 green finger chilli, finely
  chopped
1 onion, finely chopped
3 tomatoes, roughly
  chopped
½ tsp chilli powder
½ tsp ground turmeric
150ml double cream
Small bunch fresh
  coriander, roughly
  chopped
Salt

Soak the dried beans and lentils in plenty of cold water overnight. Drain, place in a large pan and add enough fresh water to cover by 5cm. Add salt, put the lid on and bring to the boil. Simmer for 2 hours. After this time, uncover and simmer for a further 1½ to 2 hours. The dal should be very tender and still quite loose, though not swimming in liquid.

Heat the butter in a large pan and add the mustard and cumin seeds. Fry for 2 minutes then add the ginger paste and green chilli. Stir for a couple of minutes and then add the onion and tomatoes. Stir until you have a smooth paste. Add the chilli powder and ground turmeric and season with salt.

Add the dal and cook uncovered for a further 30 minutes to an hour and then stir in the cream and chopped coriander and serve.

BROCCOLI WITH ANCHOVIES & CAPERS

This is a great side dish whenever you fancy doing something a little more interesting with your greens. I often eat this on toasted sourdough with a poached egg and some garlicky fried mushrooms for a tasty, meat-free lunch.

Serves 4

350g tenderstem broccoli
  or 1 large head of
  broccoli, cut into florets
1 tbsp light olive oil or
  unsalted butter
2 shallots or 1 banana
  shallot, finely chopped
1 clove garlic, very finely
  sliced
1 tsp Dijon mustard
2 tsp capers drained, rinsed
  and roughly chopped
4 anchovy fillets, roughly
  chopped
¼ tsp fennel seeds, lightly
  crushed
Small bunch flat-leaf
  parsley, roughly chopped
Salt and freshly ground
  black pepper

Blanch the broccoli in boiling salted water for about 2–3 minutes, then drain and set aside.

Heat the oil or butter in a large frying pan and, when hot, add the shallots and garlic and stir-fry for 30 seconds.

Add the mustard, capers, anchovies, fennel seeds and broccoli. Cook for 1 minute, then season to taste. Sprinkle over the parsley and serve.

CARROT & CORIANDER PURÉE

This is great served with my Achari Spiced Duck (see page 120) or try it with roast chicken, lamb or pork. The natural sweetness from the carrot balanced with coriander seeds and vinegar makes this a side dish with a difference.

Serves 4

4 carrots (about 300g),
   peeled and roughly
   chopped
200ml water
2 tsp coriander seeds
1 tbsp caster sugar
50ml white wine vinegar
2 tbsp unsalted butter,
   melted
2 tbsp fresh coriander
   leaves
Salt and freshly ground
   black pepper

Place the carrots in a pan with the water, coriander seeds, sugar and salt and pepper. Place over a low heat and cook, covered, for 15–20 minutes, or until the carrots are soft.

Tip the contents of the pan into a blender and add the white wine vinegar, melted butter and fresh coriander. Whizz until you have a bright orange, smooth purée.

CINNAMON-BRAISED RED CABBAGE

My mouth starts watering at the very thought of this – soft, slow-cooked cabbage with background notes of star anise, mace and cinnamon. You'll need a couple of hours to cook this but a good tip is to make a large batch and freeze what you don't use.

Serves 4–6

25g unsalted butter

3 tbsp olive oil

2 red onions, finely sliced

1 red cabbage, core removed and finely shredded

100ml red wine

100ml red wine vinegar

150ml water

2 Granny Smith apples, peeled, cored and cut into 2cm cubes

3 tbsp soft dark brown sugar

2 cinnamon sticks

4 star anise

2 blades mace

Salt and freshly ground black pepper

Heat the butter and oil in a heavy-bottomed pan over a medium heat. When the butter has melted add the onions and fry for 5 minutes before adding the cabbage.

Stir the cabbage well then add all the remaining ingredients. Cover and cook over a low heat for 1 hour. Check the pan after 30 minutes – if it looks a little dry add a tablespoon or two of water. If it looks too wet, uncover the pan for the last 5 minutes of cooking to allow any excess liquid to evaporate.

Remove and discard the whole spices before serving.

CAULIFLOWER & PEAS WITH CHILLI & CORIANDER

This is my mother's fantastic way of cooking cauliflower, light yet deliciously laden with flavour. Fried with ginger, garlic and spices it is the perfect accompaniment to any Indian-style curry.

Serves 4

2 tbsp vegetable oil
½ tsp brown mustard seeds
½ tsp fenugreek seeds
2 small dried red chillies
1 tsp ground cumin
½ tsp ground turmeric
4cm piece fresh ginger,
  peeled and grated
1 cauliflower (about 500g),
  cut into florets
150g frozen peas
4 medium tomatoes, peeled
  and finely chopped
Small bunch fresh
  coriander, finely chopped
Juice of ½ lemon
Salt

Heat the oil in a large, lidded frying pan over a medium heat and, when hot, add the mustard seeds. As soon as they start to pop add the fenugreek seeds, chillies, cumin, turmeric, ginger and a pinch of salt and stir with a wooden spoon for about 20 seconds.

Add the cauliflower and stir thoroughly to coat the florets with all the spices. Cook for 5 minutes.

Add the frozen peas and tomatoes, reduce the heat to low and cook for 20–25 minutes until the cauliflower is cooked through.

Stir through the coriander and lemon juice, taste and adjust the seasoning.

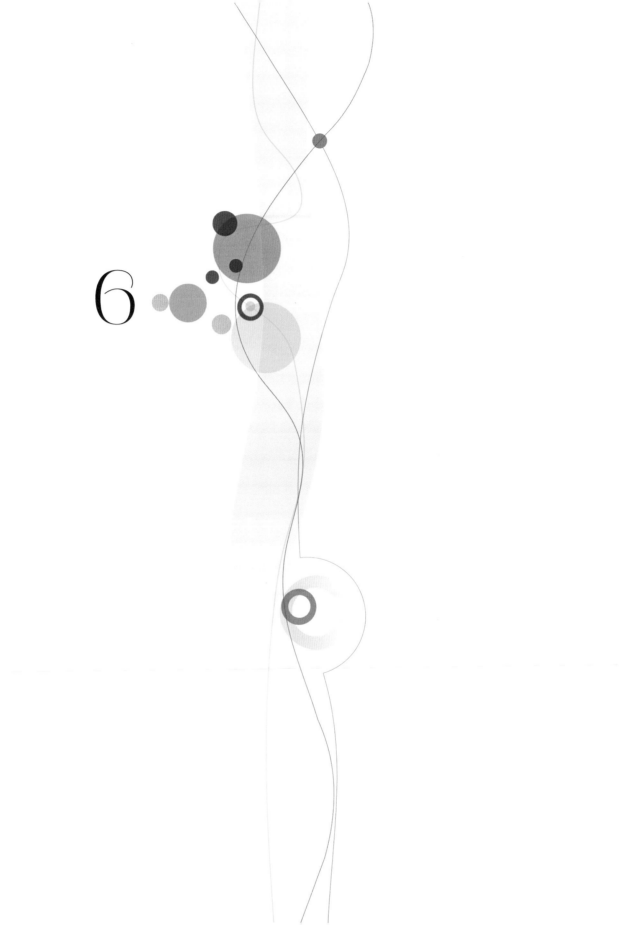

6

SWEET.

LEMON, LIME & CARDAMOM TART

Cardamom is a spice that works equally well in savoury and sweet dishes but when used in desserts like this one, you can really appreciate its floral, aromatic qualities.

Serves 6–8

For the pastry

125g plain flour

Good pinch salt

1 tbsp icing sugar

6 cardamom pods, seeds removed and finely ground

75g chilled unsalted butter, diced

1 egg yolk

1–2 tbsp ice-cold water

For the filling

6 eggs

250g caster sugar

150ml double cream

Zest and juice of 3 lemons

Zest and juice of 2 limes

First make the pastry. Put the flour, salt, icing sugar, ground cardamom and butter into a food processor and whizz until it resembles fine breadcrumbs. Add the egg yolk and water then pulse until the mixture comes together to make a firm but moist dough. Lightly shape the pastry into a disc, wrap in cling film and chill in the fridge for 20 minutes.

Roll out the pastry on a lightly floured surface and use it to line a 23cm fluted tart tin. Prick the base all over with a fork and return to the fridge to chill for 30 minutes.

Preheat the oven to 200°C/400°F/Gas mark 6.

Line the pastry case with baking paper, fill with baking beans or uncooked rice and bake blind for 12 minutes. Lift out the paper and baking beans and return the pastry case to the oven to bake for a further 5 minutes, until the pastry is pale golden and dry to the touch.

Reduce the oven temperature to 120°C/250°F/Gas mark ½.

For the filling, beat the eggs and sugar in a bowl until smooth. Stir in the cream, citrus zest and 160ml of the combined lemon and lime juices. Pour this mixture through a sieve into a jug.

Place the tart case on a baking sheet and pour in half the filling. Slide the baking sheet into the oven and carefully pour the rest of the mixture into the tart case (this prevents spillage). Bake in the oven for 40–45 minutes, until set but with a slight wobble. Allow to cool for 10 minutes and then remove the tart from the tin to cool completely on a wire rack before serving.

CHOCOLATE & CINNAMON TORTE

This torte works on so many levels: it's not overly sweet and the addition of amaretto makes it a really good dinner party dessert. It's also gluten-free but, more importantly, it tastes fantastic.

Serves 6–8

150g dark chocolate,
  minimum 70% cocoa
  solids, broken into small
  pieces
125g unsalted butter
170g light brown sugar
175g ground almonds
5 eggs, separated
200ml amaretto
Pinch ground cinnamon
200ml double cream
Icing sugar, for dusting
Raspberries (optional),
  to serve

Preheat the oven to 150°C/300°F/Gas mark 2. Lightly butter a 23cm loose-bottomed round cake tin and line the base with non-stick baking paper.

Put the chocolate and butter in a heatproof bowl and place over a pan of just simmering water. Once melted, remove from the heat and allow to cool.

Add the sugar and ground almonds to the chocolate mixture and then stir in the egg yolks, 150ml of the amaretto and the cinnamon.

Whisk the egg whites until stiff peaks form and then fold into the chocolate mixture with a metal spoon.

Pour the mixture into your prepared tin and cook in the oven for 30 minutes. Remove from the oven and allow to cool in the tin for a few minutes before turning out.

Whip the cream into soft peaks and stir in the remaining amaretto.

To serve, place a slice of torte on a plate with a spoonful or two of the cream. Dust with icing sugar and serve with a few raspberries scattered over, if using.

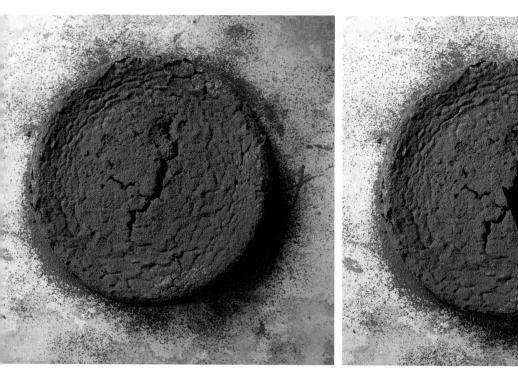

SAFFRON CRÈME BRÛLÉE

Crème brûlée is certainly a dessert worth mastering: silky smooth, rich and creamy – and who can resist the joy of breaking through the layer of caramelised sugar with a spoon? The addition of the saffron elevates this from a great dessert to one that really stands out. Serve with a decent Sauternes wine, which itself has hints of saffron.

Serves 4

600ml double cream

1 vanilla pod, split
lengthways

8–12 strands saffron

40g caster sugar, plus extra
for the topping

6 egg yolks

Preheat the oven to 150°C/300°F/Gas mark 2 and place four 200ml ramekins in a deep roasting tin.

Pour the double cream into a pan. Scrape the seeds from the vanilla pod and add to the cream along with the vanilla pod itself and the saffron. Heat gently over a low heat until almost boiling. Remove from the heat and set aside to infuse for about 5 minutes. Remove and discard the vanilla pod.

Whisk the sugar and egg yolks together in a large jug or bowl, then pour the infused cream into the sugar and egg mixture. Whisk gently to combine and then pour into the ramekins.

Pour boiling water from the kettle into the roasting tin so that the water comes about two-thirds up the sides of the ramekins. Carefully place in the oven and cook for 35–40 minutes, until set but with a very slight wobble. Remove the ramekins from the roasting tin, allow to cool and then chill in the fridge for a couple of hours.

About half an hour before serving, scatter the top of each of the ramekin with a thin layer of caster sugar. Use a chef's blowtorch to melt and caramelise the sugar. If you don't have one of these, heat a grill until very hot and place the ramekins underneath for 3–4 minutes. Keep an eye on the ramekins – you want the sugar to bubble and caramelise without melting the custard underneath.

Return to the fridge to chill until ready to serve.

WHITE CHOCOLATE & CARDAMOM MOUSSE

White chocolate and raspberries are a match made in heaven. The cardamom, with its wonderful perfume, balances the sweetness of the chocolate and the tartness of the raspberries.

Serves 4

1 sheet gelatine
1 vanilla pod, split
  lengthways
150ml whole milk
8 green cardamom pods,
  roughly bashed in a
  pestle and mortar
200g white chocolate,
  broken into small pieces
200g double cream
250g raspberries
Fresh mint leaves, finely
  shredded, to garnish

Soak the gelatine in a bowl of cold water and set aside for 5 minutes.

Use the back of a knife to scrape out the seeds from the vanilla pod and add both seeds and pod to a pan with the milk and cardamom pods. Heat until almost boiling, then remove from the heat and allow to cool for 10 minutes.

Pour the infused milk through a sieve into a non-metallic bowl to remove the vanilla and cardamom pods. Add the chocolate pieces and whisk until they are completely melted. If the milk isn't warm enough to melt the chocolate, pop the bowl into a microwave for 20–30 seconds until the chocolate is melted through the milk.

Squeeze the water out of the gelatine sheet, which will now be soft and floppy. Add to the milk and chocolate mixture and stir through; allow the mixture to cool for 10 minutes.

While the mixture is cooling, whip the cream into soft peaks, then stir the cream through the milk and chocolate.

Spoon the mixture into four glasses – I like to use martini glasses. Scatter over the raspberries and top with mint leaves. Chill in the fridge for a couple of hours before serving. You can make the mousse up to a day in advance; just add the raspberries and mint before serving.

MANGO, CARDAMOM & RUM SYLLABUB

Some recipes are incredibly simple but deliver such amazing results that they never fail to surprise me! This is exactly such a recipe and one that I make pretty much all year round – what could be better on a summer's night or cold, dark winter's evening than this reminder of more exotic places.

Serves 4

½ mango or 100ml mango
  purée
4 green cardamom pods
200ml double cream
25g icing sugar
25ml spiced rum
Juice of 2 limes
Pistachio and Cardamom
  Shortbread (see page 188),
  to serve (optional)

If using whole mango, peel and cut the flesh into chunks. Whizz in a blender, with a tablespoon of water, until you have a smooth purée.

Lightly crush the cardamom pods. Discard the husks and grind the seeds to a fine powder using a pestle and mortar or spice grinder.

In a bowl, whisk together the cream, sugar and ground cardamom until you have soft peaks. Stir in the rum and lime juice.

Stir the mango purée through the cream and pour into glasses or small bowls. Serve with Pistachio and Cardamom Shortbread for an extra special dessert.

CARDAMOM, SALTED PISTACHIO & ROSE MERINGUES

This is my twist on a classic dessert; the Middle Eastern flavours of cardamom, rosewater and pistachio transform the most English of desserts into something rather more exotic!

Serves 6–8

4–5 green cardamom pods

4 egg whites

200g caster sugar

100g salted pistachios,
  roughly chopped

½ tsp rose extract

150ml double or whipping
  cream

Few drops good-quality
  vanilla extract

200g raspberries (or other
  summer berries)

Preheat the oven to 120°C/250°F/Gas mark ½.

Grind the cardamom pods using a pestle and mortar or a spice grinder. Sieve the result, discarding the husks and fibrous bits. Set aside.

Whisk the egg whites to stiff peaks using an electric whisk, making sure the bowl is completely dry and free of any grease. Start adding the sugar, a couple of tablespoons at a time, until it is all incorporated. You should have a thick, glossy mixture.

Stir through the chopped pistachios, the sifted cardamom and the rose extract.

Line a baking tray with non-stick baking paper. Use a large spoon to drop dollops of the mixture onto the baking sheet – you should have 6–8 meringues in total.

Bake in the oven for 2 hours, until the meringues are crisp and firm. Turn off the oven and leave the meringues inside until they are completely cool.

Lightly whip the cream to soft peaks and then stir in the vanilla extract. Serve the meringues with a dollop of the cream and scattered with a few fresh raspberries. Alternatively, serve with good-quality ice cream.

The meringues will keep in an airtight container for up to a week.

RHUBARB & GINGER CRUMBLE WITH CASSIA CUSTARD

There are certain ingredients that I eagerly anticipate with the changing seasons; strawberries, asparagus, Jersey royals, cherries and rhubarb to name a few. Rhubarb is one of those superheroes that life would be immeasurably less of a joy without. The sharpness can take your breath away unless balanced with the right amount of sweetness, which here comes from the crumble and the custard.

Serves 6

800g rhubarb, trimmed
  and cut into 5cm pieces
120ml water
2 star anise
100g caster sugar
½ tsp ground ginger
1 tbsp roughly chopped
  stem ginger in syrup
4 tbsp ginger syrup (from
  the stem ginger)
150g plain flour
75g demerera sugar
75g unsalted butter

For the custard
225g double cream
225g whole milk
1 vanilla pod, split
  lengthways
2 cassia sticks
6 large egg yolks
75g caster sugar

Preheat the oven to 180°C/350°F/Gas mark 4.

Spread out the rhubarb on a baking tray. Sprinkle with water, the star anise and caster sugar and bake in the oven for 10 minutes.

Remove from the oven, discard the star anise, sprinkle over the ground ginger and mix well. Tip into an ovenproof dish and scatter over the chopped stem ginger and ginger syrup.

Put the flour, sugar and butter into a food processor and whizz until the mixture resembles fine crumbs. Sprinkle over the rhubarb and bake in the oven for 45 minutes, until the crumble topping is golden brown and the rhubarb is soft.

Meanwhile, make the custard. Put the cream and milk into a small pan. Use the back of a knife to scrape out the seeds from the vanilla pod and add these to the pan with the cassia sticks. Place over a low heat and remove from the heat just before it starts to boil.

Whisk together the egg yolks and sugar until pale and light. Strain the infused milk and add about one-fifth of this to the sugar and egg mix, whisking continuously. Slowly add the rest of the milk and cream then pour the whole lot into a clean pan. Stir continuously over a low heat until the mixture is thick enough to coat the back of a wooden spoon. Serve warm, with the rhubarb crumble.

RUM & STAR ANISE POACHED FIGS

This dessert of baked figs infused with the flavours of star anise and vanilla is delicious warm or cold. Spiced rum is widely available and gives the figs an extra hit of vanilla, cinnamon and nutmeg.

Serves 6

50ml water

50g caster sugar

2 vanilla pods, split
  lengthways

2 star anise

1 unwaxed orange

1 unwaxed lemon

25ml spiced rum

6 ripe figs

Mascarpone or ice cream,
  to serve

Preheat the oven to 200°C/400°F/Gas mark 6.

Heat the water and sugar in a pan over a low heat and stir until the sugar has dissolved. Use the back of a knife to scrape out the seeds from the vanilla pods and add these to the pan with the star anise.

Use a vegetable peeler to pare off three or four strips of orange and lemon zest and add to the syrup. Squeeze half the juice of the orange and lemon, add to the pan and simmer for about 10 minutes.

Strain the syrup into a clean pan and bring back to the boil. Remove from the heat and add the rum. Much of the alcohol will burn off but some will remain so this is one for the grown ups! Set the syrup aside.

Make a cross-shaped incision in each fig, slicing almost to the bottom but not cutting all the way through, and place in a small ovenproof dish. Pour over the syrup and place in the oven for 5–8 minutes until the figs soften.

Remove from the oven and pour over any of the juices from the ovenproof dish. Serve with mascarpone or ice cream.

RAILWAY TEA IN INDIA

The inspiration for this dish came from having travelled by train in India quite a lot as a child; 24-hour journeys across that vast country were a wondrous experience, staring out the window at the ever-changing countryside. Dusty urban sprawl would give way to open countryside, turning green in such tiny increments that you didn't realise it was happening until suddenly the scenery was lush and verdant. Those journeys were punctuated by frequent stops at the chaotic, frenetic and noisy train stations along the line. There would be coolies carrying mountains of luggage, children playing, exhausted travellers and hawkers selling everything from cheap plastic toys to steaming hot tea. This tea was the inspiration for the dessert opposite. Pale green, rubber-coated thermos flasks would be handed out and the contents poured into small glasses – the steaming hot liquid, rich with the smell of cardamom, cinnamon and a myriad of other spices would lift everyone's mood instantly.

I wanted to recreate that flavour but in a totally different way from those steaming flasks of tea from my childhood. I decided to translate the flavours into an ice cream and use that as the foundation upon which to build this dessert.

MASALA CHAI ICE CREAM WITH POACHED PEARS & CHOCOLATE TRUFFLES

The sweetness of the masala chai ice cream is nicely offset with bitter chocolate from the truffles, along with the fruity freshness of poached pears. It's quite a leap from the dusty railway stations of India but one taste of this ice cream and I can't help but smile at the memories it conjures up. Although there are several components to this dish I am asked for the recipe on an almost daily basis. Any one of the three separate elements would keep most guests happy, plus the syrup leftover from the pears is delicious added to Prosecco or sparkling wine. You will have some ice cream left over, which will keep for a few weeks in the freezer.

Serves 4

For the ice cream
1 tsp ground ginger
1 tsp ground cinnamon
Pinch black pepper
3 cloves, ground to a
  powder
350ml whole milk
1 vanilla pod, split
  lengthways
1 tsp Ceylon tea leaves
12 egg yolks
150g caster sugar
350ml double cream

For the pears
4 dessert pears, peeled
300g caster sugar
800ml water
375ml Sauternes wine
Juice of 2 oranges
2 star anise
2 cinnamon sticks
50g dark chocolate, grated
1 sheet gold leaf (optional)

For the truffles
100ml double cream
65g dark chocolate,
  minimum 70% cocoa
  solids, broken into small
  pieces
4 tbsp brandy
Cocoa powder, for dusting

First make the ice cream. Mix together the ginger, cinnamon, pepper and ground cloves and place ½ teaspoon of this mixture into a pan with the milk (store the remainder in an airtight container for another time). Use the back of a knife to scrape the seeds out of the vanilla pod and add to the pan with the tea leaves. Place the pan over a medium heat; as soon as it comes to the boil, remove from the heat. Allow to cool slightly then strain into a jug, discarding the contents of the sieve.

In a small bowl, whisk together the egg yolks and sugar until smooth. Pour one-third of the infused milk into the egg mixture, whisking continuously. Slowly add the rest of the milk mixture and transfer to a clean pan.

Place over a low heat, add the cream and stir continuously for 10–15 minutes until the mixture is thick enough to coat the back of a wooden spoon. Allow to cool and then churn in an ice-cream maker. Alternatively, pour into a shallow container and place in the freezer; after 2 hours remove from the freezer and break up the ice crystals with a fork or whisk. Cover, return to the freezer and repeat twice more.

Meanwhile, prepare the poached pears. Use a melon baller or small teaspoon to remove as much of the seeds and core from the base of the pear as possible – you want the pears to remain whole.

Put the sugar, water, wine, orange juice, star anise and cinnamon sticks into a pan and bring to the boil. Add the pears, cover with a lid and cook over a low heat for about 15–20 minutes until the pears are soft but still holding their shape. Transfer the pears along with the liquid to a bowl, cover and refrigerate.

Make the truffles by heating the cream in a pan until just simmering. Remove from the heat, add the chocolate and brandy and stir until the chocolate has completely melted. Chill in the fridge for 45 minutes. When cool and firm enough to handle, roll the mixture into small balls and dust with cocoa powder.

To serve, remove the pears from the syrup and slice a little off the base so that they stand up on a plate. Pour a quarter of the pear syrup into a small pan and bubble for 10 minutes until you have a thicker syrup and pour a little of this over each pear. (Reserve any remaining cooking liquid for the Pear and Prosecco Spritz on page 198.) Add one or two truffles to each plate along with a scoop of ice cream. Grate a little dark chocolate over the pear and top with gold leaf, if using.

KULFI

I was brought up eating kulfi and as a child I used to think that kulfi and ice cream were the same thing. Kulfi is traditionally made by heating and reducing milk, unlike ice cream, which is made from a custard and cream base. Ice cream is also churned, whereas kulfi is just frozen, which results in a denser, less airy mixture than ice cream. Here I have devised a simplified version that still delivers the flavour and creaminess of traditional kulfi.

Serves 6

1 vanilla pod, split
  lengthways
450g condensed milk
Pinch ground cardamom
300g double cream

Use the back of a knife to scrape out the seeds from the vanilla pod and add these to a bowl with the condensed milk and ground cardamom. Stir.

In a large bowl, beat the cream until it is just holding its shape and fold this into the condensed milk mixture.

Pour into individual moulds – you can buy special kulfi moulds but I tend to use dariole or ice-lolly moulds – and place in the freezer until frozen solid. Remove the kulfi from the freezer 15–20 minutes before serving.

Three variations

You can use the above recipe as a base for many other flavours. Here are three to get you started.

Chocolate

3 tbsp cocoa
1 tsp chocolate extract

Prepare the mixture as above, replacing the vanilla seeds and cardamom with the cocoa and chocolate extract. Allow to cool and then freeze as above.

Pistachio and rosewater

75g pistachios, plus extra
  to decorate
1 tsp rosewater

In a food processor, blitz the pistachios until fine. Prepare the mixture as above but without the cardamom pods and vanilla seeds. At the same time as folding in the cream, stir through the blitzed pistachios and rosewater. Freeze as above.
To serve, decorate with chopped pistachios.

Mango

1 fresh mango or
  125ml mango purée

If using a whole mango, peel and cut the flesh into chunks. Whizz in a blender, with a tablespoon of water, until you have a smooth purée.

Prepare the mixture as above but without the vanilla. Stir in the mango purée. Freeze as above.

WATERMELON, GINGER & MINT GRANITA

This is the most refreshing end to a meal you can possibly imagine, however I may be biased because I have adored watermelon ever since I was a little boy. A big wedge straight from the fridge is about as good as it gets for a five-year-old. The juices that inevitably run down your chin make this a less than appealing dinner-party dessert so I have found a way to serve watermelon in a more refined way!

Serves 8

40ml water
100g caster sugar
5–6 slices peeled ginger
1kg watermelon chunks,
   skin and pips removed
Juice of 2 lemons
2 tbsp finely shredded
   mint leaves

Put the water, sugar and ginger slices in a small pan and place over a medium heat. Stir continuously until the sugar has dissolved, then allow to cool.

Whizz the watermelon chunks in a blender and pass the pulp through a sieve. Rub the contents of the sieve with the back of a spoon to make sure you push through as much as possible. Add the lemon juice, making sure you do not drop in any of the pips.

When the syrup is cool, remove and discard the ginger slices and then stir the syrup through the watermelon and lemon juice. Add the chopped mint leaves.

Pour the mixture into a plastic or stainless-steel shallow container and place in the freezer for a few hours. Run a fork through the mixture every hour or so to break up the ice crystals. Serve in small glasses or bowls.

LEMON & CORIANDER DRIZZLE CAKE

Sweet and sharp, lemon drizzle cake is the perfect afternoon tea treat. Infusing the syrup with coriander seeds adds a wonderful citrus note that lifts an already delicious cake to new heights. I also serve this warm with crème fraîche as a dessert.

Serves 10

180g unsalted butter, softened, plus extra for greasing

250g caster sugar

3 eggs

Zest of 3 lemons and juice of 2 lemons

250g self-raising flour

1 tsp baking powder

120ml whole milk

100g granulated sugar, plus extra to sprinkle

1 tbsp coriander seeds, lightly crushed

Preheat the oven to 180°C/350°F/Gas mark 4.

Lightly grease a 900g loaf tin then line the base and sides with non-stick baking paper.

In a bowl, beat together the butter and caster sugar until light and fluffy. Add the eggs, one at a time, beating well after each addition, until you have a light and airy mixture.

Carefully fold in the grated zest of two lemons, the flour and baking powder. Gradually add the milk and mix until the cake mixture reaches dropping consistency.

Spoon the mixture into the prepared tin and bake in the centre of the oven for 50–60 minutes, or until a skewer inserted into the cake comes away clean.

Meanwhile make the syrup. Put the granulated sugar, lemon juice and coriander seeds in a small pan and place over a low heat. Simmer gently for 10 minutes or until you have a thin syrup and then strain.

Remove the cake from the oven and pierce the top all over with a skewer. Pour the syrup over the cake and leave until the cake has completely cooled. Turn out onto a plate, remove the paper and sprinkle with a little extra sugar and the remaining lemon zest.

PISTACHIO & CARDAMOM SHORTBREAD

Everyone loves shortbread and the addition of the pistachio makes it more interesting, both in terms of texture and flavour. Enjoy with a cup of tea or crumbled over vanilla ice cream.

Makes 24

90g unsalted butter, softened

40g caster sugar

5 green cardamom pods

50g pistachio nuts, finely chopped

100g strong white flour

¼ tsp salt

30g cornflour

In a bowl, beat together the butter and sugar (or use a handheld mixer) until pale and well combined.

Lightly crush the cardamom pods. Discard the husks and grind the seeds to a fine powder using a pestle and mortar or spice grinder. Stir the pistachios and ground cardamom into the sugar and butter.

Gradually add the flour, salt and cornflour, mixing gently to form a dough – be careful not to overwork the dough otherwise your shortbread will be tough. Wrap the dough in cling film and chill in the fridge for 30–40 minutes.

Preheat the oven to 160°C/315°F/Gas mark 2½.

Roll the dough out to a thickness of 1cm and cut with a biscuit cutter (alternatively just use a knife and cut the dough into rectangles).

Transfer to a baking sheet lined with non-stick baking paper and bake in the oven for 20–25 minutes, until firm and just starting to colour.

PASTRIES IN MEXICO CITY

Some of my most cherished food memories are rooted in Mexico City where I lived as a young boy. On weekends, my father would make a trip to the local bakery, bringing back freshly baked palmiers and chocolate doughnuts still warm from the oven. The palmiers were crumbly and delicious with little seams of slightly burnt sugar imparting a hint of bitterness to the sweet, flaky pastry. At the time, I was just three years old but the taste left an incredible impression on me, and I recall thinking life was pretty amazing – sitting on the kitchen bench, covered in pastry crumbs.

Years later when I went back to Mexico after my A-levels and was working at a home for street children in Atlixco, Puebla, I remember walking into a bakery on a Saturday morning and being hit with that smell of cinnamon, caramel and pastry. I was instantly transported back to being a child, excitedly tucking into the delicious treats brought home by my dad.

SPICED ORANGE PALMIERS

For this recipe, I have added a few extra flavours and have made them smaller than traditional palmiers so that they can be easily served as biscuits.

Makes 40–45

30g unsalted butter
5–6 drops orange extract
55g granulated sugar
½ tsp ground cinnamon
Pinch ground mace
375g ready-rolled puff
  pastry, cut into quarters
Zest of 1 orange
Juice of 2 oranges

Preheat the oven to 200°C/400°F/Gas mark 6.

Melt the butter in a small pan over a low heat and stir in the orange extract. Set aside.

Mix the sugar, cinnamon and mace together in a bowl. Sprinkle half onto a clean work surface and place the pastry on top. Brush the pastry with the melted butter and sprinkle with the remaining spiced sugar and the orange zest.

Starting from each long edge, gently roll up the pastry as tightly as possible until you reach the middle of the piece of pastry. Then roll from the other side so that you end up with what looks like two parallel tubes of pastry. Repeat with the remaining three pieces of pastry.

Wrap in cling film and freeze for 20–30 minutes until firm, but not frozen solid. Meanwhile, line two baking trays with non-stick baking paper.

Using a sharp knife, cut each roll into 1cm slices and place the pastry cut side up, on the baking tray, about 2cm apart. Bake for 10–12 minutes.

Meanwhile, make the glaze. Put the orange juice in a small pan and place over a low to medium heat. Simmer for about 15 minutes, until it has reduced by about three-quarters – it should be a syrupy consistency.

Remove the trays from the oven and turn the palmiers over, then return to the oven to bake for a further 2 minutes. Transfer to a wire rack and then brush the reduced orange juice glaze over with a pastry brush. Allow to cool.

7

SOMETHING

TO DRINK

MANGO LASSI

Lassi is a drink of blended yoghurt and milk and can be sweet or savoury. My father always enjoyed his lassi salted, whereas my preference is for a sweet mango lassi (pictured opposite).

Serves 4

7–8 strands saffron
4 fresh mangoes or
  500ml mango purée
800ml natural yoghurt
400ml skimmed milk
25ml caster sugar
Ice, to serve

Place the saffron in a small bowl with a tablespoon of warm water to soak.

If using whole mangoes, peel and cut the flesh into chunks. Whizz in a blender, with a couple of tablespoons of water, until you have a smooth purée.

Place all the ingredients, including the saffron soaking liquid, into a blender and whizz until smooth.

Serve in glasses with plenty of ice.

RUM & APPLE PUNCH

This cloudy apple juice spiked with fresh lime and mint muddled with dark spiced rum wins me over every time.

Serves 6–8

½ vanilla pod, split
  lengthways
1 litre cloudy apple juice
Juice of 3 lemons
Juice of 2 limes
Small bunch fresh mint,
  leaves picked
400ml spiced rum
300ml soda water
Ice
6–8 cinnamon sticks,
  (optional) to serve

Use the back of a knife to scrape out the seeds from the vanilla pod and add to a large jug or punch bowl with the apple juice, lemon and lime juice, mint leaves, rum and soda water. Stir well.

Serve in tall glasses filled with ice and, if using, decorate each glass with a cinnamon stick – it can act as a stirrer but also slowly adds a wonderful cinnamon flavour!

PEAR & PROSECCO SPRITZ

I created this recipe by accident, as a way of using up the leftover syrup from the poached pears on page 179, but I liked it so much that I turned it into a recipe in its own right. Use the syrup recipe here or the one on page 179 if you are making that – both will keep well in the fridge for a couple of weeks, meaning you can have instant cocktails – just add fizz.

Serves 6–8

For the syrup

200g caster sugar

500ml water

2 cinnamon sticks

Zest and juice of 2 oranges

Zest and juice of 2 lemons

1 tsp cardamom pods

2 large ripe pears, peeled
  and cored

1 bottle Prosecco or other
  sparkling wine

1 bottle sparkling water

Mint sprigs, to serve
  (optional)

Put all the ingredients for the syrup into a pan and place over a medium heat; stir until the sugar has dissolved. Reduce the heat to low and simmer until the liquid has reduced by half – about 15 minutes. Allow to cool.

Strain into a jug and discard the contents of the sieve. At this point, the syrup can be transferred to a bottle and stored in the fridge until ready to use.

To make the cocktail, put two tablespoons of syrup into the bottom of a champagne flute. Add enough sparkling water to come a third of the way up and top up with the Prosecco. If using, add a sprig of fresh mint to each glass.

CARDAMOM MARTINI

A good martini needs to be made using the best ingredients possible, as there is nowhere to hide. Vodka or gin, mixed with vermouth, ice, a twist of lemon zest and some crushed cardamom pods produces a cocktail that is bone dry and undeniably grown-up.

Serves 4

150ml good-quality
  ice-cold gin or vodka

1 lemon

Large handful of ice

75ml dry vermouth

6 cardamom pods, bashed
  in a pestle and mortar

I always keep gin and vodka in the freezer to ensure my martinis are ice-cold – the alcohol stops it freezing completely. I also put the martini glasses in the freezer 20 minutes or so before I need them.

Use a sharp knife to pare off four slices of lemon rind to make 'twists' or cut four thin slices from the lemon.

Place the ice in a cocktail shaker with the gin or vodka, vermouth and cardamom. Shake for 30 seconds, then strain into four glasses. Garnish with the lemon twists or slices and enjoy – I strongly suggest you don't have more than one before dinner!

CINNAMON & STAR ANISE HOT CHOCOLATE

Hot chocolate can lift the spirits almost instantly. To boost the feel-good factor even more, I have included a couple of my favourite spices: cinnamon and star anise. For a grown-up version, add a glug of Drambuie or Cointreau.

Serves 4

900ml whole milk
1 cinnamon stick
1 star anise
½ vanilla pod
200g dark chocolate,
  minimum 70% cocoa
  solids, broken into small
  pieces
150ml single cream
1 tbsp caster sugar
100ml Cointreau or
  Drambuie (optional)

Heat the milk in a pan with the cinnamon stick, star anise and vanilla pod. Bring up to a simmer then remove from the heat.

Strain about a quarter of the milk into another pan and then whisk in the chocolate until you have a smooth, thick, glossy mixture. Strain the rest of the milk into the chocolatey paste and stir until it is all mixed in.

Stir in the cream, sugar and booze (if you are making the grown-up version). Serve piping hot.

MASALA CHAI

Perfectly sweet and laden with layers of spice, this is truly one of India's signature flavours. Masala chai varies enormously throughout India and can include ginger, cardamom, cinnamon, cloves – even black pepper.

Serves 4

600ml whole milk
3 tsp black tea leaves
5 tsp caster sugar
2 cloves
8 green cardamom pods
1 cinnamon stick
Generous grating of
  nutmeg
½ tsp black peppercorns

Place all the ingredients in a pan and gently bring up to the boil. Allow to simmer for 5 minutes, stirring occasionally. Strain into mugs or tea glasses (to make it really authentic) and enjoy.

MULLED CIDER

This has become a family tradition on bonfire night. Lighter than mulled wine but with just as much depth of flavour, it is also delicious served chilled with lots of ice, a sprig of mint and a slice of lemon.

Makes 1 litre

750ml dry cider
250ml cloudy apple juice
Zest of 1 lemon
Zest and juice of 1 orange
1 tsp cloves
3 cassia or cinnamon sticks
2 star anise
4 tbsp caster sugar
50ml calvados or apple
  brandy

Mix all the ingredients together in a heavy-bottomed pan and heat gently while stirring until the sugar has completely dissolved.

Just before the mixture comes to the boil (steam rises from it and tiny bubbles appear around the edge of the pan), reduce the heat to very low and leave for a further 10 minutes, taking care not to let it boil or even simmer. Remove from the heat.

Strain into a heatproof jug and serve immediately.

8

RELISHES

& ACCOMPANIMENTS

KACHUMBER

A cross between a salad and a salsa, this is a delicious and fresh accompaniment to a hot curry. It's particularly good with Yellow Pork (see page 70).

Serves 4

4 ripe tomatoes, diced
½ cucumber, peeled, seeds removed and diced
1 red onion, finely chopped
Juice of 1 lime
1 green finger chilli, finely chopped (I leave the seeds in for an extra kick)
½ tsp caster sugar
¼ tsp ground cumin
5 tbsp finely chopped fresh coriander
Salt and freshly ground black pepper

Put all the ingredients together in a bowl and mix until well combined. Taste and adjust the seasoning. Chill in the fridge for an hour or so before serving to allow the flavours to meld together.

GUACAMOLE

The key to good guacamole is to use ripe avocados. If your avocados are too hard, just wrap them in newspaper or place in the fruit bowl alongside some bananas and they will ripen in a couple of days. I usually make this to go with Turkey Mole (see page 115), but it also makes a great snack with warm pitta bread or tortilla chips.

Serves 4

2 large ripe avocados

1 medium red onion, finely chopped

2 tomatoes, roughly chopped

1 green finger chilli, seeded (optional) and finely chopped

Juice of 1 lime

2–3 tbsp extra virgin olive oil

Salt and freshly ground black pepper

Halve and stone the avocados, then use a tablespoon to scoop out chunks of the avocado flesh into a bowl.

Add all the remaining ingredients and stir carefully to combine. Don't overmix as you don't want the avocado to turn into a paste. Taste and adjust the seasoning.

CUCUMBER RAITA

I am often asked how you can tone down a dish that has too much heat in it. The answer is not easily ... but a good solution is to serve this refreshing raita – the cucumber and yoghurt work wonders to douse those chilli flames! This is also a tasty dip for everything from vegetable crudités to fried fish.

Serves 4–6

1 medium cucumber,
  peeled, cut lengthways
  and seeds scraped
  out with a spoon
500ml Greek yoghurt
½ tsp caster sugar
¼ tsp salt
½ tsp ground cumin
Juice of ½ lime

Grate the cucumber using the coarse side of your grater – try and grate it lengthways so that you end up with longer strands of cucumber.

Mix all the remaining ingredients together in a bowl.

Squeeze as much liquid as possible out of the cucumber and add to the yoghurt mixture in the bowl. Stir well to combine. If it feels too thick add a little water. Chill until ready to serve.

MINT & CORIANDER YOGHURT

You find this eaten all over India – it works well with almost any dish. Serve with grilled or barbecued meat, use in wraps or as a dip with crudités.

Serves 4

1 tsp garlic and ginger
  paste (see page 215)
1 green finger chilli,
  seeded (optional) and
  finely chopped
½ tsp caster sugar
Juice of 1 lime
Small bunch fresh
  coriander, leaves
  and stalks
Small handful mint leaves
50ml water
250ml Greek yoghurt
Salt and freshly ground
  black pepper

Place all the ingredients except the yoghurt and salt and pepper in a blender and whizz until you have a smooth, dark green paste.

Stir through the yoghurt, season to taste and serve.

TAMARIND YOGHURT

Panch puran is a blend of spices primarily used in east India. Here, it works particularly well with the flavour of tamarind in a delicious yoghurt. It is perfect with any fried seafood dish or my Crab Cakes (see page 31).

Serves 4

100g tamarind pulp

500ml just-boiled water

2 tsp caster sugar

200g Greek yoghurt

Juice of ½ lemon

Salt and freshly ground
   black pepper

For the panch puran

1 tbsp fennel seeds

1 tbsp black mustard seeds

1 tbsp cumin seeds

1 tbsp nigella seeds

½ tsp fenugreek seeds

First make the panch puran. Lightly toast all the spices in a dry frying pan. Allow to cool before coarsely grinding, using either a pestle and mortar or a spice grinder. Store your panch puran in an airtight container and use as required.

In a small bowl, soak the tamarind pulp in the water for 25–30 minutes. Pass through a sieve, discarding the seeds, and pour the pulp into a small pan.

Bring to the boil and then add 1 teaspoon of the panch puran and the sugar and allow to simmer, stirring often for about 15 minutes, or until reduced by two-thirds.

Pass through a sieve again and allow to cool. Mix with the yoghurt and lemon juice. Season to taste and serve.

CHOUCROUTE

A classic dish from the Alsace, this is essentially a kind of pickled cabbage. The cabbage is cooked in an array of spices, along with wine and vinegar, giving a fabulous sharpness. Store in an airtight container in the fridge for up to a week and enjoy with cold meat – it's perfect in a cold roast beef sandwich.

Serves 6 as a side dish

25g unsalted butter

1 white cabbage, very
   finely shredded

150ml white wine

100ml white wine vinegar

50ml water

3 cloves garlic

1 sprig fresh thyme

3 bay leaves

7–8 juniper berries

1 cinnamon stick

2 star anise

5 tbsp caster sugar

Melt the butter in large, lidded pan over a medium heat and when foaming, add the cabbage. Cook for a couple of minutes, stirring constantly, then add the wine, vinegar and water.

Add all the remaining ingredients, cover and simmer for about 1½ hours, stirring every 10–15 minutes. The cabbage should be soft and all the wine and vinegar should have evaporated – if it dries out before the cabbage is soft, add a little water and continue cooking until it's ready.

Serve immediately, taking care not to bite into the spices, or allow to cool and store in the fridge.

PLUM & BLACK CARDAMOM SAUCE

Fruit-based sauces are excellent paired with richly flavoured game – here the black cardamom adds an unusual smokiness. This sauce can be served hot or cold and is particularly good packed in a picnic to liven up a pork pie.

Serves 4–6

250g plums, halved and
  stones removed
2 black cardamom pods
2 cinnamon sticks
1 tsp paprika
4 tbsp soft dark brown
  sugar
200ml water
1 tsp fennel seeds
20ml sherry vinegar

Put all the ingredients in a pan and place over a medium heat. Stir until the sugar has dissolved and then cook, covered, for 20 minutes.

Remove from the heat and pass the contents of the pan through a sieve (use the back of a wooden spoon or ladle to push as much as possible through). Return to the pan and then simmer on a low heat for 10 minutes to thicken further. You should end up with a glossy syrup, which coats the back of a spoon.

SHALLOT PURÉE

This simple purée is rich, creamy and luxurious and will add a touch of decadence to almost any meat dish. I adore it with beef and use it as I would a béarnaise sauce – with grilled lamb or roast chicken.

Serves 4

25g unsalted butter
150g banana shallots, very
  finely sliced lengthways
1 sprig of fresh thyme
1 tsp fennel seeds
75ml double cream
Salt and freshly ground
  black pepper

Melt the butter in a frying pan and add the shallots, thyme sprig and fennel seeds. Cook over a low to medium heat for about 25–30 minutes. The shallots should be soft and a pale golden brown colour.

Add the cream and simmer for about 10 minutes, until reduced by half. Remove and discard the sprig of thyme.

Pour the whole lot into a blender and whizz until silky smooth – you want the smoothest purée possible. If you still have a few bits left after blending, use a spatula to pass the purée through a fine sieve. Season to taste.

TOMATO RELISH

Tangy and sweet with an added kick from the spices, this is a delicious accompaniment to many dishes, or simply as a spread in sandwiches. I love this with barbecued meat.

Serves 4

500g tomatoes, chopped

1 large onion, finely chopped

2 cloves garlic, finely chopped

1 roasted red pepper, chopped

1 red chilli, roughly chopped

100ml white wine vinegar

85g soft brown sugar

25g sultanas

1 tsp black mustard seeds

½ tsp nigella seeds

1 tsp smoked sweet paprika

1 cinnamon stick

6 cloves

Salt and freshly ground black pepper

Place all ingredients in a large pan, cover and cook over a low to medium heat for 30 minutes. Remove the lid and cook for a further 20–30 minutes or until the liquid has evaporated and you have a thick, chutney consistency.

Allow to cool, then remove the cinnamon and cloves and serve. This will keep in the fridge in an airtight container for up to 2 weeks.

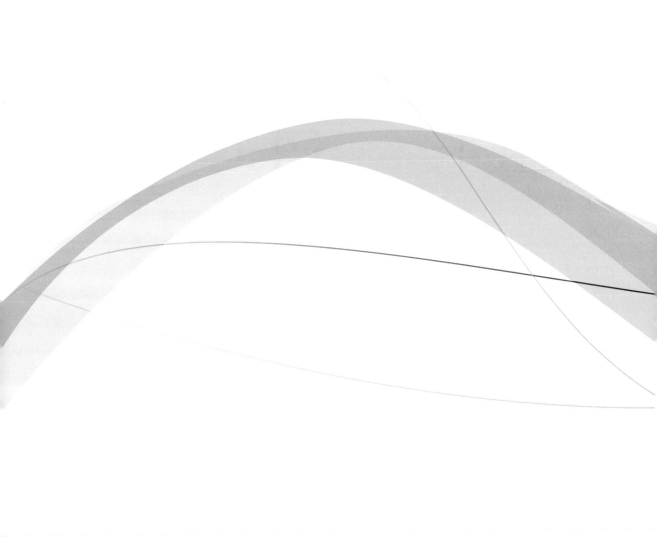

UNLOCKING THE
SPICE CUPBOARD

SPICE GUIDE

The idea of using spices can be daunting, overwhelming even. The sheer number of them is a lot to take in and then there are the individual characteristics of each one to contend with. Below is a list of the spices I cook with most often along with information about what they look like, how they taste, how they smell, what they go with and how best to cook with them.

Cooking with spices is more art than science and so it is impossible to make purely objective. Spices are like living things: they have personality, a soul. Having the skill to combine them in the right way will bring dishes to life but you might find it helpful to know a little bit about their characteristics and what kind of flavours they bring out.

Most of the spices you will ever need are easily available from your local supermarket but visit specialist shops if you are looking for obscure ingredients. Indian food shops offer pretty much everything you might need spice-wise, even those not really associated with Indian cookery. Another great place to look is in large Chinese supermarkets.

If you have a decent coffee grinder, spice mill or a pestle and mortar, get maximum flavour out of your spices by grinding them from whole as and when you need them. It might even be worth investing in a small coffee or spice grinder especially for this purpose. Ready-ground spices do have their place though – the important thing is to look after them to lock in their flavour.

SPICE CARE

To extend the shelf life of your spices ensure they are kept away from heat, moisture and sunlight. Try not to leave either whole or ground spices unused for more than 3–4 months. It's best to keep them in a cupboard or drawer, rather than right by your cooker or stove. Buy small glass, plastic or metal sealable jars or tins and label them. I would love to say that my spice cupboard is beautifully tidy and clearly labelled but it isn't – a real case of do as I say, not as I do!

Ajwain seeds

Also known as carom seeds, these contain hints of thyme with a menthol note and a slight but pleasant bitterness. They are similar in appearance to cumin seeds but are shorter and rounder. Used widely in Indian food, ajwain seeds are often one of the spices added to hot oil to make *tadka* (see page 219).

Allspice

I used to think that allspice was a blend of spices but it is actually the dried unripe fruit of the West Indian allspice tree, so-called because it contains hints of cinnamon, cloves, nutmeg and pepper. It's most often used in Caribbean cookery, most notably jerk chicken, but is also very good in desserts.

Asafoetida

This unusual, pungent-smelling spice is the ground, dried resin that comes from the roots of a herb, which grows mainly in Afghanistan. Sparingly used, asafoetida adds a unique savoury note to dishes, especially lentil dishes or Achari Spiced Duck on page 120.

Bay leaves

Bay leaves might not seem as exciting as some of the sexier spices such as star anise or vanilla but they are essential to so many of my recipes. Use fresh or dried bay leaves but the flavour is more mellow in the dried version – crush one between your fingers and you will notice the faint aroma of eucalyptus and a pleasant floral note. They are most often used whole to flavour sauces and casseroles or to infuse milk when making a béchamel sauce.

Caraway seeds

This spice really divides opinion. I have to admit that I am not a great fan but those who like it, love it. Sharing some of the same flavour properties as cumin and aniseed, it is one that is quite powerful and easy to identify. Often appearing in rye bread it is also used to flavour liqueurs, Dutch cheeses and desserts. It appears in many northern European cuisines, particularly in Scandinavian breads and liqueurs, but can also be found in Middle Eastern and Indian cooking.

Cassia

Also known as Chinese cinnamon, this has a much more robust flavour than cinnamon and is thicker in appearance. It is incredibly versatile and as good in savoury dishes (biryani, moussaka, casseroles) as it is in sweet dishes (ice cream,

mulled wine, panna cotta). I often use cassia instead of cinnamon because it tends to hold its shape, unlike cinnamon bark. It has a sweet, warming and menthol-like aroma.

Cardamom pods (black)

These are dried and smoked over an open fire to give them that wonderful smoky flavour. They have a camphoric aroma and should be used sparingly to add a unique dimension to meat stews, rice dishes and sweet fruit sauces. I can't help smiling when I think of black cardamoms as they remind me of my childhood when family meals were invariably punctuated by my dad finding one of these in his food by biting into it and rendering his palate useless for the remainder of lunch.

Cardamom pods (green)

Known as the queen of spices, cardamom is both sweet and savoury in character. It has notes of lemon, ginger, rosewater and cinnamon so is often used in desserts. Use cardamom whole to impart flavour (pick out the pods before serving) or lightly crush and grind the seeds to a powder (see Lemon, Lime and Cardamom Tart, page 162).

Chilli powder

From India, there are mild, medium and hot chilli powders as well as Kashmiri chilli powder, which is a much deeper red but milder than the other varieties. I tend to cook with dried Kashmiri chillies as they have a sweeter flavour and provide that beautiful red colour. Cayenne pepper, used more widely in the Americas, is a good substitute.

Chinese five-spice powder

As the name suggests, this is actually a blend of spices used all over China and South East Asia. Traditionally it was made up of cloves, cinnamon, fennel seed, star anise and Sichuan peppercorns, but nowadays can also include liquorice root, ginger and nutmeg. It was initially designed to deliver all five taste sensations – sweet, sour,

213

salty, bitter and pungent – so really does add an amazingly rounded flavour to dishes.

Cinnamon

Nothing evokes Christmas more than the warming and comforting aroma of cinnamon but I cook with cinnamon all year round and probably use it at least two or three times a week. It is equally at home in savoury or sweet dishes and is used in Chinese, Indian, Moroccan and Spanish cuisines. As with cassia, use the sticks whole to infuse slow-cooked dishes or ground cinnamon to give a subtle hint of flavour, such as in my Cheat's Moussaka (see page 92).

Cloves

This pungent aromatic spice can easily overpower dishes – cloves are rarely used as a primary flavour and work best with other spices. They are found in garam masala and in Chinese five-spice. Cloves have a hint of sweetness and menthol and can have a numbing effect on the tongue – the reason why they are often used to ease toothache – so take care to pick whole cloves out of a dish before serving! Infusing milk with onion, bay leaves and a couple of cloves gives an interesting, more rounded flavour to béchamel sauce (see Cauliflower Cheese with a Cumin and Macadamia Crust, page 132).

Coriander seeds

These ridged, light-brown seeds have an amazingly complex aroma: woody, floral and citrus at the same time. They are the dried fruits from the same plant from which we get coriander leaves and also coriander blossom. If I am using coriander seeds with red meat I toast the seeds in a dry frying pan for a few minutes – the flavour changes dramatically, becoming more earthy, smoky and nutty. However, if I am cooking fish or poultry I leave them untoasted, as the citrusy, floral notes tend to disappear after dry roasting. I always add a couple of teaspoons to homemade

fish stock, when making apple sauce to serve with pork and insist on a generous amount of them in my mulled wine at Christmas. Don't be limited to using them just for savoury dishes (see my Lemon and Coriander Drizzle Cake, page 186).

Cumin seeds

These have one of the most distinct flavours of all the spices and are used all over the world. The Dutch flavour cheese with it, it's one of the most widely used spices in Indian cuisine and you will also find it used all over North Africa. Cumin has a deep, earthy, woody aroma but is incredibly aromatic. The seeds smell totally different when dry roasted in a pan – they become much more nutty and some of the fragrant floral notes disappear. Cumin can be used ground or as whole seeds. Mix with ground coriander, chilli powder and turmeric to make a very simple spice mix as a base for curries.

Curry leaves

I adore curry leaves. They are best used fresh (look for them in Asian food shops) but you can also freeze them to use later – simply place in an airtight container or strong plastic bag. Dried curry leaves simply don't have the same strength of flavour. Fresh leaves have an exotic, lemony aroma but they also have a warming smell – like watercress or mustard. Curry leaves are flash-fried in hot oil to get the most of their intoxicating and nutty fragrance (see note on Tadka, page 219).

Fennel seeds

These have an unmistakable anise-like flavour and are slightly sweet with a hit of fresh woodiness and a delicious floral quality. Anise, fennel seed and tarragon all feature in my cooking because of those wonderful heady notes I associate with fennel. Fennel seeds are used in everything from French to Italian cooking, as well as Chinese five-spice powder. Fantastic with fish and vegetables, they also work wonderfully with pork.

Fenugreek seeds

These dull yellow, angular-shaped seeds have a very distinct musky, slightly bittersweet flavour that should be used sparingly. Also known as methi, try dry roasting them to intensify their wonderful nuttiness and to tone down the bitterness. They are usually roasted and then crushed or ground but are also used whole as a pickling spice. Fenugreek leaves, though more of a herb than a spice, are widely used in Indian cooking and can be used fresh or dried – I tend to use them dried as they are packed with flavour and have a lovely grassiness (see Beef Fillet with Fenugreek and Potato Crust, page 98).

Galangal

A rhizome just like ginger or turmeric root, this is an ingredient used all over South East Asia. It has a more floral aroma than ginger, along with a peppery and almost citrus-like flavour. It is available fresh, dried or in powder form but I only use fresh galangal – you can find it in Asian grocers so buy a large quantity and freeze it for another time. Try it in my Duck Braised with Star Anise, Soy and Galangal (see page 116).

Garam masala

A spice mix usually consisting of some of or all of the following: cinnamon, black peppercorns, cumin, nigella, cloves, nutmeg, mace, green cardamom and black cardamom. In Hindi 'garam' means hot and 'masala' means 'spice' but here hot doesn't mean chilli heat – it refers to the heating effect that certain spices have on the body according to the Ayurvedic system. The garam masala mix varies enormously from region to region and even household to household! I have a few versions depending on what I am using it for – the spice blend for meat dishes would be deeper and more intense than the ratio I would use for fish and seafood.

Ginger

This knobbly looking rhizome is used all over the world in many different guises. Fresh, dried, powdered, candied; the list goes on. From the same family as galangal and turmeric this is the daddy of them all. In its raw form, it boasts bold, fiery flavour, which smells as amazing as it tastes. Fresh ginger crops up throughout the recipes in this book – it's readily available and will keep for several days in a cool, dry place. I often add a few slices to stocks and broths but most of the time it is peeled and then grated or used as a paste. A good tip is to peel a large amount of ginger and then whizz in a food processor with a splash of water. It freezes well in ice-cube trays, meaning you will always have a ready supply of **ginger paste**. Many of my recipes call for **garlic and ginger paste** – this is simply a 50:50 blend of peeled garlic cloves and peeled fresh ginger. Whizz in a food processor, again with a tablespoon or two of water, and freeze as for ginger paste.

Harissa

This complex spice mix from North Africa is sweet, sharp and hot and contains a wonderful mix of spices – cumin, coriander and caraway among others. It is most often used in paste form and is widely available from good supermarkets. It is often used with lamb but I love it with fish, as it enhances the natural sweetness of seafood. Use it to rub over fresh sardines (see page 52) or mix with yoghurt and fresh mint for a simple but delicious marinade for salmon.

Juniper berries

I came to juniper quite late in life – it's more of a northern European spice, whereas I grew up in Mexico and India. It is very aromatic with hints of pine and can also be quite bitter. I use the berries whole – my two favourite dishes using juniper are Spiced Confit Duck with Pistachio Nuts (see page 118) and Choucroute (see page 207).

Kaffir lime leaves

These beautiful dark green, hourglass-shaped leaves are used extensively all over South East Asia. They add a prodominantly citrus flavour, which is much more floral and perfumed than you would get from lime zest. Kaffir limes themselves are incredible (a gin and tonic with kaffir lime is a thing of joy) and nowadays you can buy them easily. Look for fresh leaves in Asian food stores and freeze any you do not use for another time.

Lemongrass

Elements of lemon and lime zest, galangal and floral notes make lemongrass a very special ingredient. It is an integral part of big, bold fiery dishes like Beef Rendang (see page 95) but is also equally at home playing a much more subtle, delicate role, such as in Thai Veal Salad (see page 88). If you are finely chopping lemongrass you will need to remove the tough outer layer first, but if adding whole stalks to soups or stews, simply bruise it by bashing the stalk with the back of a knife. Lemongrass stalks make great skewers for koftas, kebabs or large prawns when barbecuing. They freeze well, too.

Mace

Mace is the outer husk of nutmeg and has a similar flavour profile, although more peppery and less sweet. Mace blades can be used whole or toasted and ground to a fine powder – although you can also buy mace as a ground spice.

Mustard seeds

Mustard seeds come in several colours – yellow, black and brown – each with their own characteristics and differing in aroma and taste. All mustard seeds pop when added to very hot oil, releasing their flavour. **Yellow mustard seeds** have a creamy nuttiness and a hint of raw pea flavour but also an underlying bitterness. Often crushed and mixed with a little water to form a paste in cooking. **Black mustard seeds** are stronger in flavour than their yellow and brown counterparts and as such should be used more sparingly. I tend to only use these as a spice rather than trying to turn them into a paste because you end up with a nutty and slightly bitter flavour without any of the creaminess. If paired with curry leaves and/or coconut, as in Malabar Prawn Curry (see page 54) or Green Beans with Coconut (see page 148), they give a stunning flavour. **Brown mustard seeds** are the most widely used – they come from a different plant to yellow or black mustard seeds and are not as pungent as black mustard seeds although they have a very similar flavour profile.

Nigella seeds

These tiny jet-black seeds have a smoky, slight bitterness to them, not too dissimilar to thyme and oregano. Also known as black onion seeds they are used as a pickling spice and are often sprinkled on top of naan bread – their slightly bitter taste contrasting with the sweet bread.

Nutmeg

Originally from Indonesia, nutmeg is now grown all over the world and used in both savoury and sweet dishes from Japan to Malaysia, India, North Africa, Europe, the Caribbean and the Americas. I first saw nutmeg growing in Mauritius at the Pamplemousses Botanical Garden – so valuable are these crops that each plant was encircled by iron fences to keep inquisitive cooks like myself away from the precious crop. The round, yellow faintly plum-like fruit burst open to reveal the nutmeg inside, encased in the bright red lacy covering, which is dried to give us mace. Although nutmeg is available ready-ground, whole nutmeg can be easily grated. Its sweet, nutty, slight cinnamon flavour enhances anything from béchamel sauce to a custard tart.

Pepper

The most widely traded and used spice in the world, this is indeed the king of spices. Most varieties of peppercorn (green, red, white and black) come from the same plant and are merely the fruit at varying stages. Pink peppercorns, however, are from a different plant altogether. Peppercorns are used whole to infuse dishes with flavour or ground to give a warmth to food. White peppercorns are essentially black peppercorns that have had their outer skin or husk removed. The flavour of white pepper is slightly less robust than black pepper, making it ideal for delicate sauces such as hollandaise, béarnaise or mayonnaise.

Ras el hanout

This spice blend is originally from Morocco but is now used all over North Africa. There is no definitive recipe – it can be made from up to 50 different spices including chilli powder, coriander seeds, cumin seeds, green cardamom, cinnamon, black pepper, cloves, ginger, mace, nutmeg and turmeric, to name a few. It is used to liven up tagines, rubs, marinades and braised dishes but my all-time favourite is with lamb (see page 84).

Saffron

Saffron consists of the dried stigmas of the crocus *sativus* and is the most expensive of all the spices – more valuable by weight than gold. This is because each stigma is hand-picked and a high volume of flowers will only yield a tiny amount of strands. Ninety per cent of the world's saffron comes from Iran but is it also grown in India and Spain. Saffron imparts a stunning, deep ochre colour to dishes. Often recipes will tell you to soak the strands in a little milk or water, to help activate the strands and extract the colour. It has a faintly metallic smell, almost like chlorine, with a hint of grassiness but this transforms into the most divine flavour and smell when used properly. Use it sparingly as it can easily overpower other ingredients. Saffron is a key ingredient in bouillabaisse, paella and biryani but it can be used in plenty of other ways: a pinch of saffron added to a garlicky aioli transforms it into the most stunning golden sauce perfect for dipping crisp fried seafood into (see page 47).

Star anise

Visually one of the most beautiful spices. They are most commonly associated with Chinese cookery but are also found in the cuisines of South and South East Asia. Each perfectly symmetrical with its eight points, each concealing a shiny seed. They have a versatile aniseed flavour but also a sweetness as well as a hint of liquorice. It is one of the ingredients of Chinese five-spice powder and is amazing when rubbed over duck before roasting but I think it comes into its own when used whole to impart that fantastic flavour to dishes. Like nutmeg or cinnamon, it is equally suited to sweet or savoury food.

Sichuan peppercorns

This is an amazing spice, its uniqueness coming from the numbing effect it has on your mouth. It is fragrant with citrus notes (a cross between dried orange peel and lemon zest) and there is initial warmth followed by a tingling sensation and an almost menthol-like, cooling effect. One of the components of Chinese five-spice powder, it also works well on its own.

Tamarind

I was brought up around tamarind and its many uses both in Mexico and India. It is generally used as a souring agent thanks to its sweet and sour flavour. Inside the pods is a brown, sticky pulp containing seeds – you can find the pulp in Asian food stores, vacuum-packed in plastic. This pulp needs to be soaked in water and then passed through a sieve to create a paste, although you can also buy ready-made paste. In Mexico the paste is sweetened and used to make cold drinks, ice lollies and granitas as well as in cooking. In India it appears in the curries of south Indian, especially Keralan fish curries.

Turmeric

Turmeric is a key spice in the Ayurvedic system of medicine but is equally important in the kitchen. It is a rhizome, similar to ginger or galangal, but is bright orange inside – when dried this root turns bright yellow and ground turmeric has a really earthy, slightly mustardy smell and adds depth of flavour as well as the most beautiful colour to dishes. If you are lucky enough to get hold of fresh turmeric root, that's another beast altogether – giving you the same earthiness along with a freshness and delightful floral note. However, ground turmeric is perfectly acceptable for the recipes throughout this book.

Vanilla pods

These pods cultivated from the vanilla orchid were first introduced to Europe by Hernán Cortés, following the discovery of the Americas in the 1500s. Their deep, rich, sweet aroma and flavour immediately captured the hearts and taste buds of those important or wealthy enough to be lucky enough to try them. Although more accessible today, vanilla still has that effect on people. The long, shiny dark brown pods contain millions of tiny vanilla seeds – to extract them slit the pod lengthways and scrape them out with the tip of a knife. They are usually added to sweet dishes but try my Vanilla Mash (see page 133) for something different. This is a pretty expensive ingredient so don't waste anything – the used pods can be used to flavour sugar in airtight jars. Good-quality vanilla extract is a good alternative.

THE MANY WAYS TO USE SPICES

Having learnt a little more about the different spices available, you can try out my recipes with confidence. But what if you want to experiment on your own? Spices can be used in different ways to add flavour to a dish, and how you use them in a recipe will depend not just on the spice itself but on what you are cooking and how you are cooking it. Here are a few ways that I have used spices in the recipes.

Whole spices to infuse flavour

The beauty of many spices is that they can simply be added whole to dishes and left to do all the work. I add whole cinnamon sticks, star anise, cloves and dried chillies to slow-cooked dishes, stocks and casseroles, while cardamom pods, bay leaves and cloves can be added to milk for deliciously flavoured béchamel sauce, ice creams and any number of desserts.

Dry roasting whole spices

Many spices, such as cumin or coriander seeds, completely come to life after being toasted in a dry frying pan – the heat releases the aromas and intensifies the flavour, giving dishes an almost smoky finish. Dry roasted spices can then be crushed or ground and added to sweated onion and garlic to form the basis of any number of curries.

Frying spices in oil

Certain spices, such as mustard seeds, are traditionally 'popped' in Indian cooking to release new dimensions of flavour – they are usually thrown into hot oil at the beginning of a dish. The technique known as *tadka*, where spices such as mustard seeds and curry leaves are fried in oil and tipped over a finished dish just before serving, is also widely used, particularly in southern India – often for making dals.

Making marinades and rubs

These are two very simple ways to add flavour to your dishes. Both whole and ground spices can be added to oil or yoghurt to make delicious marinades for meat, fish and vegetables – left for several hours the flavours have time to develop. One of the quickest ways to add spice to your cooking is to combine ground spices, often with a little salt, and use to rub over meat or fish before cooking – perfect for barbecues or grilling.

Making flavoured butters

Flavoured butters are a great way to use spices and the beauty is that they can be kept in the freezer for several weeks. Use ground spices or dry roast and grind your own and combine with finely chopped fresh ginger, coriander, mint – the possibilities are endless. Shape your flavoured butter into a sausage shape, wrap in cling film, freeze and then simply cut off a round as and when you need it. Perfect for pan-frying a simple fillet of fish or a steak.

INDEX

Page numbers in *italic* refer to the illustrations

ACKNOWLEDGEMENTS

This book would simply not have been possible without the help and support of several people whom I owe a lot to on a daily basis.

Mum and dad for giving me every opportunity a son could have wanted – from amazing childhood holidays right through to the constant support you give me, without which I couldn't do half the things I do. I can't thank you both enough.

Aileen, my amazing wife. Thank you for allowing me to follow my dream and for putting up with everything that this has meant over the past few years. You have been more supportive and helpful than I thought possible and for that I am eternally grateful.

To the MasterChef family for making my dreams of a career in food a reality. John and Gregg for having the unenviable task of choosing between Tim, Alex and me. Karen, Dave A, Dave C, Nozzer, Katie A, Lou and Bev and the series six team – thank you.

To my friends who are always there to reassure me on those off days, who remind me I have made the right decision and make me proud of the food I cook – there are many, but my wonderful friend and incredibly talented cook Lisa, aka Princess Pixie, gives me constant support and reassurance. My good friend, mentor, sounding board and beacon of good advice, John Torode. Thank you JT.

To Amanda Harris at Orion who had the faith and belief in my food to make this book a reality and to Kate Wanwimolruk for your help and guidance in ensuring it fulfilled its potential. Thank you so, so much.

Lizzie Kamenetzky, food stylist extraordinaire, but more importantly, dear friend: I am in awe of how you manage to make food look good and without you this book would have not been a patch on the final result. Crucial team members, Polly Webb-Wilson, Kate Whitaker and David Eldridge – working with you guys was a pleasure and a joy and I was so lucky to have your expertise on this book. I can't imagine working with anyone else!

Thank you for letting my book happen. A book I have always wanted to write but never would have without all you wonderful people.